"LOOKING DOWN THE YEARS"

EXETER - THE HELFORD - PLYMOUTH COMMAND

1919 - 1945

First published 1996 by
BUTLER BEACHAM
April Cottage, Otterton, Devon EX9 7HB
Telephone 01395 568849

Copyright © Nora Butler 1996

ISBN 0 9528421 0 6

All rights reserved. No part of this book may be reproduced or transmitted in any form or by any means including recording or photocopying, without permission in writing from the publisher.

Printed by B.P.C. Wheatons Ltd
Hennock Road, Marsh Barton, Exeter, Devon EX2 8RP
Telephone 01392 420222

Copies of this book may be obtained from The Exeter & District Hospice, Dryden Road, Exeter EX2 5JJ, Telephone 01392 402555, or from Butler Beacham, Otterton

Front cover
"When we were very young"
Shrimping at Exmouth, c. 1922

Back cover photo by Alan Quincey
The Authoress

Cover design by Alan Quincey

"LOOKING DOWN THE YEARS"

EXETER - THE HELFORD - PLYMOUTH COMMAND
1919 - 1945

A Memoir
by
Nora Butler

INTRODUCTION AND ACKNOWLEDGEMENTS

To my friends on the Fund Raising Committee of Budleigh Salterton & District Hospiscare, I dedicate this little book.

"Looking Down The Years" is a memoir of my life from 1919 - 1945, the story of an ordinary girl who, after a happy upbringing in the ancient city of Exeter, lived through the extraordinary years of the War; first at the famous Ferry Boat Inn on the Helford River, and later in the W.R.N.S.

I owe many thanks to Jill and Bruce Beacham, and to Alan Quincey, for their patience and computer skills in preparing the book for the printers, and to Harry Sharpe and Ben Gorner of B.P.C. Wheatons Ltd for their help and encouragement.

Liley Cooke lent the Primrose Pitman engraving of the pre-blitz Exeter High Street, Maud Rickards the picture of the young Deacon Rickards, and the Express & Echo gave permission for the reproduction of the picture of the site of the old Bedford Circus. I am indebted to Derek Carter for photos of Commander Gerard Holdsworth, Pierre Guillet and the French tunnyman 'Mutin' which was part of the Helford Flotilla.

Nora Butler, May 1996

"LOOKING DOWN THE YEARS"

EXETER - THE HELFORD - PLYMOUTH COMMAND
1919 - 1945

CONTENTS

PART I - AN EXETER CHILDHOOD

Chapter 1	Early Days in the Twenties	7
Chapter 2	Growing Up in the Thirties	29
Chapter 3	Work at The Fisherman's Cot at Bickleigh Bridge	35
Chapter 4	Clouds of War	39
Chapter 5	Blitzkrieg and The Dunkirk Miracle	50

PART II - THE HELFORD RIVER

Chapter 6	Life at The Ferry Boat Inn	53
Chapter 7	The Battle of Britain	61
Chapter 8	Carrying On	65
Chapter 9	The Unspeakable Haw-Haw	67
Chapter 10	Foreshadows of Death	69
Chapter 11	The Helford Flotilla	78
Chapter 12	A Visit from The General	84
Chapter 13	Farewell My Friend	87
Chapter 14	Enchanted Summer	90
Chapter 15	Killerton, a Tranquil Interlude	96

PART III - PLYMOUTH COMMAND

Chapter 16	Bombed out at Mannamead	101
Chapter 17	D Day	104
Chapter 18	Teignmouth	106

Clockwise from the left: John, Bruce, Marjory, Molly, Freda and Nora in 1930

PART I - AN EXETER CHILDHOOD

Chapter 1 - Early Days in the Twenties

The Great War to end all wars came to an end in September 1918. I was born a year later in September 1919 and twenty years after that, in September 1939, the second Great War broke out. Thus all my growing up was between the wars, the two greatest world-shattering events of all time, but it didn't prevent me having a wonderful childhood. There was actually a strike taking place while I was being born and for several days, milk was unobtainable. My Mother told me in later years she feared I would starve to death but I survived.

For my parents, Ellen and Frederick Reynolds, this must have been a very happy period in their lives for there was still a certain amount of euphoria in the air after the war and my Father, newly demobbed, was so delighted to be reunited with his wife and three children that I was conceived quite soon after his return.

As a married man with a young family, he had not at first been called up, but volunteered in late 1915 when a plea went out for men who could drive. It was for a secret project. This turned out to be the formation of the Tank Corps and he was one of the first five hundred members. They trained on Salisbury Plain, learning to deal with these extraordinary vehicles which were expected to change the whole conception of warfare. In fact, they had little impact as the brass hats with the cavalry traditions couldn't conceive a suitable strategy for these new-fangled monsters and a great initiative was lost by the Allies. The Germans of course quickly cottoned on to their potential and perfected their blitzkrieg tactics in time for the second conflagration. Many are the times I have heard Father inveighing against the generals who fought a twentieth century war with nineteenth century minds.

We grew up with stories of dreadful disasters and bloody victories, of Ypres, Vimy, the Somme and Passchendaele, ringing in our ears. He was fortunate to survive, having endured several poisonous gas attacks and escaping on one occasion from a blazing tank just before it exploded. These experiences left him unscathed physically but Mother said he was affected emotionally for some time. He became a chain-smoker and his somewhat mercurial temper became positively incandescent, and he also acquired a picturesque vocabulary, quite new and shocking to her ears. Nevertheless, he was still a kind and charming man and a loving Father, despite Victorian notions of discipline. Mother was of a very different temperament, more serious, very practical, less mercurial and humorous, her feet firmly planted on the ground. They complemented each other and were wonderful parents to the six offspring they eventually produced, despite the difficulties of the times.

Just in time for my appearance in the world, Father bought a large Victorian terraced house called Trevone in Exeter. Our neighbours were pretty tolerant but I think Mother lived in constant dread of our noisy ways causing offence. Usually we were kept under pretty firm control but we certainly had our moments, particularly when John and then Freda arrived and our parents were out and we were left in Mrs Mainford's care.

We all adored "Mayday" as my older sister, Molly, dubbed her. She had a great sense of humour and of the dramatic, and we hung on her every word as she told us wonderful gory stories about the war and of famous crimes, floggings and hangings. She had boot-black hair, owing more to art than nature I suspect, as it was never grey, high-coloured cheeks and thin features. Her hands, though beginning to suffer from rheumatism, were still dextrous and she had, for us, magic corns on her feet which could foretell rain more accurately than modern weather-forecasters. But her great feature was her laugh, a cheery, raucous cackle which we tried to invoke as often as possible. She told us of her childhood, of her hard-working Father, a jobbing tailor, and of her schooling for which she paid sixpence a week. He didn't send her to the State schools which had been set up under the 1870 Act.

Mrs Mainford came with the house. "I'll never forget seeing your Father for the first time," she used to tell us. "So pleased he was to be home from the war. I was scrubbing the kitchen floor when he came in and jumped right over my bucket!" "You must be Mrs Mainford," he said. "I have just bought the house and heard nothing but good about you. Will you stay on and help my wife?" "So I looked up at him, so young and debonair he was, and I just said, 'well, all right sir. If your wife and I seem to suit, I'll stay on for a while'. I still come, don't I, despite all you young varmints."

She was a war widow with two young sons. I expect her pension was a few shillings a week and she earned enough to bring them up by "doing" for various folk. Her home was one of a row of tiny cottages, two up and two down, with a strip of garden for vegetables and Mayday being Mayday, she always seemed to have a row of bright flowers. I expect it was damp, but it always seemed so cosy and welcoming. Bill, her older boy, was quiet and serious, while Jack, the younger, was the apple of her eye, and had her marvellous sense of humour. Alas, she was to lose him in a swimming accident at Trews Weir. It wasn't actually an accident - he picked up typhoid and died. It was a terrible tragedy which we all felt keenly and she didn't sing and laugh very much for a long time. Fortunately Bill proved a very good son; he was never married and looked after her until she died well into her eighties.

I think Mrs Mainford and her ilk were the salt of the earth with their fortitude, their courage, their kindness and their ability to make so much out of so little. They are a dying breed. We all learned so much from her, not only practical skills but insights into social conditions that we would otherwise never have obtained.

I suppose this was a general happening, and the relationship between servants and employers was an important educational fact years ago, a process of osmosis whereby each learned something from the other, widening horizons, learning about differing social conditions, cherishing and passing on the domestic wisdom of the ages. Certainly she taught me the art of pastry-making. From her, together with Mother, my sisters and I learned the rudiments of home-making.

Mother's generation was probably the last of the professional home-makers. Their homes were their kingdoms, impeccably managed, cosy, clean, welcoming. "You have a duty to yourself, a duty to your family and a duty to society," was her dictum. She brought us up, ran the home, was a companion to my Father and always did her share of charity work, and her friends shared similar ideals.

Trevone was a typical example of its period, built about 1870. There was a small front garden with steps to an entrance porch which gave onto a smallish hall. On the left was the door to the drawing-room, straight ahead was the staircase with its four flights of stairs and to the left of the staircase, the kitchen passage, the dining-room to the left with french doors to a courtyard, and the kitchen, scullery and a larder ahead. The back garden was walled in and very safe for children. Mother gave up attempts at garden-making - she put geraniums in the courtyard and the rest was laid to grass, with a rather unhappy flower border. We had small plots in the old vegetable garden which we sowed with marigolds and cornflowers. The glory of the garden was an ancient cherry tree. It was a froth of white blossom in the spring and always bore a good crop of White Heart cherries, but it also had a sturdy branch which supported a hammock where many a lazy hour was spent reading or dreaming youthful fantasies. Beyond the garden was the maze of back lanes which led to the tradesmen's entrances of each house. Beyond the back lanes was the market garden which was bounded by the Great Western railway line to Torquay and Plymouth.

We were great railway buffs and knew all the names of the famous steam engines and many of the drivers who would acknowledge our waves and cheers. These were the days of the Cornish Riviera and the Torbay expresses, with their luxury pullman cars. In hot summer weather, "sixpenny specials" were run from Exeter to Dawlish and Teignmouth and the trains would be absolutely crowded with cheering, hot and dusty city workers, thankful for the chance of a few hours by the sea. The rail network was very responsive to the needs of passengers in those days and we adored travelling by train. There were plenty of porters to help with the luggage and the station masters in their magnificent gold-braided uniforms paraded the platforms, holding large watches to check arrival and departure times.

After a long journey, Mother always took us to thank the train driver and his fireman. If we were lucky, we might be lifted up onto the footplate to see the red-hot firebox and the gleaming array of levers. The drivers were the kings of the railways, but the guards were in overall charge of the trains and so reliable that from the age of seven, I travelled to Tunbridge Wells in the charge of the guard. In London he would escort me to the Tunbridge Wells train where my grandparents would meet me.

Mother used to say she didn't know how she would have managed us all without Mayday. She found a little resident maid and advised on trades people and kept the monthly nurse happy when first I, and then John and lastly my sister Freda were born. We were the post-war brood, Molly, Bruce and Marjory having arrived in 1912, 1914 and 1916.

I can remember Freda's arrival quite clearly. Marjory, John and I were puzzled by the air of turmoil in the house. It was more like washday with the copper boiling away in the scullery, but Mayday seemed less patient than usual and kept trying to stop us from going upstairs. Mother, apparently, wasn't very well. I managed to escape and nearly got into her bedroom when a large, strange nurse quickly brushed me away and I retreated upstairs to the playroom. Big sister Molly scolded me for being disobedient and tried to entertain we younger ones but we were not in a mood to be amused and accused her of being bossy. Then Father came bounding up the stairs in great excitement and told us we had a brand new baby sister. Oh, what joy! We clambered up onto the big bed and surveyed the enchanting bundle in Mother's arms. Oh, what magic! Our very own little baby in our very own house! Father took the little bundle from Mother and bade us get off the bed as he gently crooned and showed her off to us. Dr Stokes packed his little black bag. He patted Mother and murmured something about tomorrow, and the large nurse beamed in the background. Mayday came into the crowded room, dabbing her eyes with the corner of her apron and Mother smiled the serene, triumphant smile of motherhood.

I have never forgotten that smile but I had never really understood it until my own son was born some twenty years later.

Big sister Molly was very possessive of the new arrival. She was a marvellous older sister and I regarded her as a fount of wisdom but we only saw her in the holidays. She had been left behind in Tunbridge Wells when Father returned from the Great War. When Father had left originally, my Grandmother Clarke had been horrified at the idea of my Mother being left alone in the wild and woolly West Country with two small children and a third on the way. She made Grandpa drive her down from Kent, scooped them up from their lovely little Devonshire home and took them back to Tunbridge Wells. Once she got them there, I don't think she quite knew what to do with them as Mother was the only married one of her six children, and though Engadine was a commodious residence, it wasn't made of elastic. Three extra souls placed quite a strain on its resources, particularly when sister Marjory started to make an unexpected early arrival into the world and Mother had to be rushed into a nursing home on the eve of her sister Ethel's wedding. Eventually Mother managed to find a little flat near my grandparents' house. Brother Bruce settled down quite well but Molly was emotionally disturbed by all the upheavals. The doctor suggested school and she was enrolled into the kindergarten at Tunbridge Wells High School at the early age of four and a half. She seemed to settle very well, so it was thought inadvisable to uproot her yet again in 1919 and she remained at the High for the rest of her school days, living with Granny and Grandpa Clarke during termtime and coming home for the holidays.

Mother, Father and Freda at Engadine, 1927

Molly has since told us how she hated being separated from the family and Mother sadly missed her oldest child but thought it was for the best. Thus, they both suffered unnecessarily through the lack of communication between generations which was fairly common before the last war. Molly had a great gift with the young and to this day is a much-loved granny and a popular great aunt to my own grand-daughters.

We really looked forward to her holiday visits. We had a large playroom at the top of the house and when she was at home, we were allowed to have an open fire up there where we spent long cosy winter days when it was too cold or wet for much outdoor activity. But we didn't often escape the afternoon walk, however inclement the weather. What a buttoning of gaiters! What a lacing of boots! What a hunting for mufflers and gloves! We were probably out for only three quarters of an hour. Years later, I asked Mother why she bothered. Well, she and other mothers of that time could teach Dr Spock and the other specialists a thing or two about child management. "Don't you see?" she said, "it probably took half an hour to get you all ready, then, even if we were only out for thirty minutes, a lot of fizz can be walked off in that time out of doors. It took another half hour to get you all undressed again and then you could go and watch for the lamplighter until tea was ready." Oh, the lamplighter! He was indeed one of our delights! A rather small man with a very long pole, he walked robustly down the road in the 'dimpsey', twitching his hook and leaving soft golden pools of gaslight in his wake, and if perchance the muffin man came along, pealing his bell and crying out "Hot muffins!", our cup was not only full but running over. Is there anything more appetising than toasted muffins after an invigorating walk on a cold December day?

Actually, as we got older, we really were unholy terrors, particularly when our parents were out. I remember one night we were all supposed to be in bed but it was a fine light evening, too good to be wasted. Big brother Bruce came upstairs and led us to the balcony overlooking Alphington Road. The open-topped double-decker trams ran down the middle of the road and, by taking careful aim, we could blow orange pips through homemade paper tubes right among the startled passengers. Tiring of this little ploy, we spotted a lady in a large flower-decked hat just about to walk under our balcony. "That herbaceous border needs watering," Bruce muttered as he emptied a glass of water over the unfortunate woman. We heard the front door bell ring furiously. "Someone upstairs has just poured water all over me. I have a good mind to fetch a policeman," said the irate victim. We were leaning over the stairwell so we could hear the conversation. "Never," said Mrs Mainford, "not my children. Perfect little ladies and gents they are, and they are all asleep anyway. They wouldn't dream of doing such a thing." Wouldn't we just? Perfect little horrors we were! I dread to think what we might have done had we not had firm parents.

I remember another occasion when I was annoyed with my brother John. I threw a book at him. He ducked of course and the book went right through a big plate glass window on the landing. Of course, I got into terrible trouble and then I blamed him for ducking. After that, my conscience smote me and I realised I really had got to curb my temper. My brothers and sisters used to call me "pepper pot" and after that I really think I began to get a little nicer and less explosive.

Mayday came along twice a week, on Mondays and Fridays. Monday of course was wash day. What a to-do! First the copper had to be lit, then the dirty linen sorted and boiled in the steaming cauldron. It had to be rinsed by hand, then blued and finally mangled and hung out to dry. While the boiling went on, the more delicate articles of wool and silk were hand washed and the rather dreary Monday lunch prepared. Finally the copper was emptied and the scullery scrubbed with hot water. Actually, we all hated Monday, particularly as we grew older and trudged the two miles home from school for a lunch of cold meat and boiled potatoes, boiled rice with jam and the smell of boiled clothes all over the house. Even Prudence, our beloved alsatian, would desert the steamy scullery and station herself at the top of the first flight of stairs whence she could instantly see us coming through the front door, and would rush down to greet us in rapturous welcome.

It was a great day for Mother when the Beeston boiler was installed in the kitchen to supply constant hot water, but I think Mrs Mainford and the current maid were even more delighted when, later on, the old copper was removed from the scullery and replaced with a gas one.

On Friday Mrs Mainford would help with turning out the main bedrooms. This was a very great laborious business. All the ornaments had to be piled on the bed and covered with a old sheet. Then the carpet was hand-brushed with washed tea-leaves to lay the dust. Then everything had to be polished and put back, and then Mayday would cook the lunch so that Mother could spend the morning shopping. Most things could be obtained in Alphington Street near at hand, but certain items Mother liked to buy in the city and after all, it was as good an excuse as any for a morning off. During the holidays we often accompanied her. First stop would probably be at the Devon & Somerset Stores in the High Street. Mother would sit down with the Provision Manager while he brought her joints of bacon and samples of cheese for her inspection, and she would say "Well, I'll have two pounds of that best Wiltshire back. It looks very good. And two pounds of the streaky. And I'll have two pounds of Cheddar cheese, and half a pound of the Stilton. I think I'll have two pounds of New Zealand butter and a pound of the Devonshire." Then there would be lard and all sorts of other things, and then we would go on to the Dry Goods Department where she would have Mazawattee tea, Demerera sugar, dried fruit, patna Carolina rice, tinned peaches for some special treat, and some hard tack biscuits of which we were very fond. In the spring there would be isinglass for egg pickling and in the winter, almonds and spices and raisins for the Christmas cakes and puddings. Very few items were prepacked. Everything was deftly ladled out of the large green canisters decorated with gold, and everything was weighed on shining brass scales and put into paper bags of various hues to denote the contents. I particularly remember that pale blue was for sugar and dark blue was for currants.

The tiny Empire Cinema was next door to the Devon & Somerset Stores and we would take a quick peek at the photos displayed outside.

Cinema-going was a rare treat for us and we were never allowed to see a film that hadn't been vetted by Father or Mother.

Miltons the Chemists was probably the next port of call. We liked Mr Milton and went to kindergarten with his sons. His shop, like all pre-war chemists shops, contained a fascinating array of large glass containers filled with coloured water, and there were rows and rows of mahogany drawers, labelled with mysterious names like "Ipecac." Again, most things were carefully weighed on small scales in drams and ounces, or measured into bottles. There was Glycerine of Thymol for sore throats, Iodine for cuts and grazes, Arnica for bruises. There was Vaseline and boracic lint and various widths of bandages. There was tooth powder for us all, shaving sticks for Father, smelling salts for Mother and lavender toilet soap for the whole family.

Mother would gaze rather longingly at the gorgeous creations in Joan Cresswell's elegant gown shop, or she might go into Brufords Antique Department for a word with her great friend, the silver-haired Mr Andrews, who was their antiquarian. Then she would cross the road to Paynes' Coffee Shop. Every morning the High Street was filled with the aroma of Paynes' roasting coffee beans which in spring mingled with the scents from the flower sellers' trays. The whole street was alive with colour and activity.

High Street, Exeter, before the Blitz.
(Primrose Pitman engraving)

The old trams clanged down the rails in the centre between streams of cars and vans and horsedrawn vehicles going in both directions. Bicycling errand boys whistled gaily - they knew all the latest popular tunes - and the sandwich-board men walked up and down advertising the latest films or posters saying "Prepare to Meet Thy God". There were balloon sellers and purveyors of small, bewildered tortoises. There were street photographers, lace sellers and, very sadly, ex-servicemen with trays of matches and pins or small performing toys. I think the newspaper sellers amused me most with their cries of "Press'nEchoo" which was the Express & Echo, the local paper.

There was no television of course and few people even had wireless sets so that there were many 'extras', perhaps comprising a single sheet with the latest cricket or football results. The Oxford and Cambridge Boat Race always received an 'extra', such was the enthusiasm for the event, and everybody wore light or dark blue rosettes, according to their favourites.

From Paynes', we would probably go into Bobbys elegant store if Mother required bed linen or tablecloths, and then to Dingles which was called Colsons in those days, where she would go for dressmaking materials, haberdashery or an occasional new hat. She was a wonderful dressmaker and made all our dresses, even our school uniforms. She was very up-to-date with her dressmaking. She had dispensed with all the petticoats which most little girls wore in those days and she made our frocks with matching knickers so that we still looked respectable, even when we did handstands!

If there was time, we might be treated to coffee milk at Dellers, the famous, beautiful restaurant in the old Bedford Circus, the beautiful Regency circus which was completely destroyed by the Blitz. And then we traipsed down to Stillmans the butchers in South Street where she would buy enormous joints of meat.

We would arrive home to the delicious aroma of Mayday's lunch which was very different from the austere Monday meal. She made delectable pastry and to this day we all talk of her chicken and rabbit pies and her mouth-watering casseroles. If Father was at home she would beg Mother to go and play for him to sing. "Ada and I'll dish up, Mrs Reynolds. We'll be quicker if we have some music." She would let out her famous laugh. Mother would seat herself at the small Broadwood in the drawing room and Father's fine baritone would ring through the house, echoed by Mayday's more raucous tones from the kitchen.

We always looked forward to Saturdays. The boys had to go to school of course. School in the morning and they had to play games in the afternoon, but we girls were able to stay at home. For some time we had a pleasant trustworthy maid called Kitty and she often took us out if we didn't want to accompany our parents. A favourite haunt was the canal and there were many pleasant places to picnic in the sunny water meadows between the river and the manmade waterway. Many small trading vessels used the waterway. A number of them were sailing ships which were hauled by horses, beautiful patient plodding Shires, one on each bank attached by ropes to the ships which drifted peacefully between them. One day we watched horrified as a drunken skipper steered his vessel so erratically that one of the poor beasts was pulled into the water. Despite the united efforts of the drovers and spectators, the beautiful creature was drowned and we were so upset that we didn't visit the towpath for some time after that.

Exeter viewed from the canal

  The basin and the river quay was a very happy hunting ground for my brother Bruce. He passed that way to Exeter School, crossing the river by the chain ferry to the old Custom House on the quay, and from thence to Colleton Crescent and Barrack Road. He got to know the captains of the regular ships and chatting to them opened up a new window on his world. He picked up all sorts of information which was passed on to the family at meal times. Indeed, later on in the thirties, I think this was the first time we received our inklings of the coming troubles from Germany. Many of the ships came from Northern Europe and the Baltic area and they told of the massive build-up of the German Navy. Bruce had an adventurous character. He was intelligent enough but not naturally studious and there was usually trouble when his reports came in. 'Doesn't try hard enough'. 'Could do much better if he kept his brain in the classroom' etc. He was avidly interested in Scott and Amundsen and in all stories of exploration, and complained to Mother one day that by the time he grew up, there would be nothing left unexplored, nothing new to do.

  Our beloved alsatian Pru accompanied us on most of our expeditions and Mother used to say that she was as good as a nanny. Certainly no one could have harmed us when she took us in charge. There is no doubt that she was one of the gentlest and most beautiful bitches I have ever known. She never had to be told anything more than once. Indeed, she seemed to anticipate our wishes and was ever obedient. She would take the newspaper from the letterbox each morning and deliver it at Father's bedside. She would fetch his slippers for him and she would never dream of eating her dinner until given permission, even when it was put under her nose. If we forgot to feed our little guinea pigs, she would bark and scold until we prepared the bran and lettuce leaves and then she would accompany us to the hutch to make sure we did the job properly. In return, she expected to be treated as one of the family. She would bring in her bowl and drop it at Mother's feet when tea was being poured, putting a gentle reminding paw on Mother's lap until the bowl was filled.

One day she appeared on the stage in a school rendering of Red Riding Hood. She made a marvellous wolf, lying on a bed with blankets tucked round her, one of baby sister's frilled bonnets on her head and spectacles on her long nose. At the appropriate moment we called out her one hate-word 'cats!' and she jumped out of bed and chased Red Riding Hood right across the stage. Her performance brought the house down and she was voted the star of the show. We all loved her dearly and if we were in trouble for some childish misdemeanour, we could always find comfort lying against her satin neck with one of her paws around us.

Nora, Pru, Freda and John
Butterleigh Bridge 1930

Father was usually at home at weekends and if not playing tennis or cricket, would sometimes take us to his small factory where soaps and washing powders were produced. One of the best sellers was called Domexe. It was in tablet form and its great selling point was its easy solubility in cold water. Comparatively few people had constant hot water in those days and to be able to soak soiled linen in cold water and Domexe and have it emerge sparkling white was wonderful. Shampoos, scouring powders and an excellent chilblain ointment were other products. We found the upstairs packing room fascinating, with cheerful white-clad girls laughing and chatting away as their nimble fingers wrapped and packaged the various products.

The manufacturing was carried out on the ground floor, reached by a rather rickety ladder. Here were huge boilers and mixing vats and apparatus for filling tins and packets. Big double doors led to a yard with surrounding storerooms and garaging for the delivery vans. The Manager was a nice man called Mr Curnow. He used to give us pennies as he escorted us round, so he became high in our pantheon of heroes.

Sixty years or more ago, a large proportion of our national output came from these small, labour-intensive manufacturers but they were finding it an increasing struggle with the large number of bigger companies. Father's bête noire was Messrs Lever Brothers, who achieved market share with massive advertising and rather inferior raw materials. Father had a chemist friend, a sort of consultant I suppose, and they were always experimenting with new formulae which received their final tests at Trevone. We would all be very interested and help with suggestions for suitable names and packaging designs. If a product pleased Mother and Mayday, this was considered its final accolade and it quickly went into production.

With his ever-increasing family, Father must have been under intense pressure to provide for us all and in time, he took on the South West agency for Brand's, the high-class food manufacturers, famous for their A1 Sauce and excellent tinned meats and invalid foods such as calves' foot jelly and chicken essence. I have never tasted tinned salmon like Brand's Canadian Sockeye, or such excellent ready-made soups. The turtle soup was superb, made from turtles kept alive in special tanks until required. I remember being taken on a tour of the factory in Vauxhall and my feelings of distress on being shown the poor turtles swimming around in their tanks. But their keeper was a nice man who went to great pains to keep them healthy. There was a large temperature gauge at the side of the tank to keep a constant temperature, and he told us that specialists from the zoo advised on diet. "But what about the poor salmon?" I asked anxiously. "They would hate to be confined like this." "Oh, they are processed as soon as they are taken from the Sockeye River in Canada, and then shipped over here," Mr Brady the Sales Manager explained to us. He also was a great friend and came to see us often.

Brand's went to enormous trouble to produce the very best quality foodstuffs and were asked by the wartime Food Ministry to pioneer the new concept of baby foods, which was so important during the war when food was difficult and babies' nutrition was so important. Father's success with Messrs Brand's prompted him to turn part of his factory into a wholesale food warehouse and he secured the English agency for a famous Dutch chocolate maker. For a while it was hugely successful, and as children we revelled in this latest product. Then, once more, disaster struck. The General Strike in 1929 prevented supplies getting through from Holland. Father tried importing by aeroplane, at that time a very daring thing to do, but the strike went on too long and it proved hugely expensive. Another initiative was stifled.

But despite all the setbacks, he managed to provide for us all and got us all properly educated. You either got on or went under in those days. There was no state aid to bale you out. Families stuck together. Wives supported their husbands when times were difficult.

After Saturday came Sunday, which we found a great bore. It was the lifelessness, the air of solemnity which hung like a pall over pre-war towns and cities, that dampened our Sunday spirits. However, if the weather was good and we could escape to beach or countryside after the traditional Sunday roast, we would be as ebullient as ever. We attended Matins at what was referred to as The Tin Church in Willey's Avenue, so called because of its corrugated iron roof. In wet weather the rain pattering on the roof competed with the voice of the curate in charge and the music squeezed from the ancient harmonium, but we all preferred this funny little church to the fine red sandstone parish church. It was bright, airy and intimate I suppose, and nearer home. Though I had a fervent belief in God, I disliked going to church. I thought life was wonderful, full of joy and colour and excitement. I couldn't understand why we should sit in a gloomy church, thinking about death and going to heaven when life, wonderful life, was throbbing just outside the door.

My first visit to the Cathedral changed all that. It was a revelation - my first spiritual experience, a feeling of being part of something so much bigger and greater than myself, a transportation to another sphere. It was the music of course, the angelic purity of the choirboy voices harmonising with the crashing chords of the organ, and then the joy of joining in with the congregation in an ecstasy of glorious sound.

Sunday afternoons in winter could be fun. We read or sewed or played dominoes in the drawing-room by the glowing open fire. My parents were very enlightened and there was none of the nonsense about not doing sewing or anything useful on a Sunday. We had grown-up tea using the best china and silver tea service and afterwards, Mother might play the piano for hilarious sing-songs, or Bruce would entertain us with snippets from Chaucer. He read the Old English very well and I used to be entranced, transported to another age, another world of shadowy figures with strange ways and an extraordinary manner of speech. All too soon, bedtime arrived and then it was 'back to school' Monday and washday blues once again.

We attended Edgerton School in Pennsylvania Road some two miles from home. This arrangement came about when brother Bruce was due to start his education. Our neighbour's daughter was driven to the kindergarten at Edgerton each morning and they kindly offered to take Bruce with her. Mother and Father approved of the scheme of schooling provided so we were all enrolled in due course. The boys proceeded to Exeter School when old enough, while we girls went on to the upper school at Edgerton.

Apart from a firm grounding in the three R's, one of Bruce's first accomplishments was to learn knitting. He produced a set of dark green woollen reins and one of my earliest recollections is of swinging around on the end of them as he led me about. One winter's day I got fed up with thus being restrained. He wouldn't let me go so I seized his brand new gloves and I managed to escape long enough to push them into the letterbox at Ide. Bruce thought it uproariously funny but Mother was not at all amused. My impulsiveness and high spirits constantly led me into scrapes. Indeed, Mother said I was the most trying one of the family to control in early childhood, but all that changed after a term or two at school and I became most horribly priggish.

One morning as I lurked around the parental bedroom, hoping for a sip of early tea, I noticed some crayon marks on the satin striped wallpaper. "What naughty little girl did that?" I enquired primly. "You did," said Mother, "the very first day it was pasted. Now stop dawdling in here and go and get dressed. Don't forget your teeth and don't forget to wash behind your ears." Bloodied but unbowed, my hot little hand was soon clutched in sister Marjory's and we set off for Edgerton. We boarded the tram at Exbridge and disembarked in High Street, opposite the old arcade, then we walked down Longbrook Street, up Pennsylvania Hill and into the school cloakroom to start another scholastic day.

I was thrilled when old enough to travel backwards and forwards on my own. I wandered all over the city, even venturing into forbidden slum areas which were at last being cleared and the inhabitants moved into newly-built council housing estates. One day I ventured down Bartholomew Street, an attractive but very run down area where many families were crammed into the ancient houses. I always entered this area with a slight apprehension as there were usually gangs of ragged urchins about, who would boo and even throw stones at anyone in a school uniform. I found aniseed balls a great weapon in these circumstances. We each received a penny a week for pocket money. Though I disliked aniseed balls, they represented good value at twenty for a penny. I usually invested in a ha'penny's worth and one day, on being chased, I threw some at my persecutors and made a getaway as they stopped to pick them up. On one occasion, instead of the usual gang, one solitary boy sat alone on the pavement. His dirty face was creased with tears. "Can I help you?" I asked politely, because my heart smote me. I really felt sorry for him. "Garn," said the boy. "Mind your own business," or words to that effect. I felt helpless but dearly wanted to do something. My fingers touched on a solitary toffee nestling in my pocket. I took it out and placed it carefully by his side. "Get off with you!" shouted the boy, so I took to my heels, but when I glanced over my shoulder, I was delighted to see that he was unwrapping the sweet.

This incident worried me. For the first time, I actually realised the meaning of dire poverty and I told Father about it when I got home. "Why are some people rich and some people poor?" I wanted to know. "Oh, you're growing up," he said. "I wish it wasn't so. It makes me furious when I think of the terrible poverty cheek by jowl with Buckingham Palace, but I don't honestly know what can be done about it except to give all one can to try and alleviate the worst effects. The extraordinary thing is that some people rise to great heights from very humble beginnings. We all have free will you know. I think as much depends on willpower as upbringing, but there's no doubt a good home gives a child a good jump-off. Always remember that and be thankful, and remember that from those to whom much has been given, much will be expected."

On school days we went home for midday lunch, thus travelling some eight miles a day, most of it on Shank's pony. If we wanted to save money for birthday or Christmas presents or Marjory wished to buy flowers for her current favourite mistress, we walked the full distance to save our tram money of tuppence a day. My legs were shorter than Marjory's and I got very tired but if she was in a saving mood, she was relentless. I was jolly glad when I was considered old enough to go alone as I have already said. I could walk at my own speed and explore where I liked, a feeling no doubt experienced by sister Freda when she started out under my protection. Instead of lollipop persons, the policemen who were on point duty shepherded children across dangerous spots in those days. The overall volume of traffic was nothing like it is today but there weren't the number of roads either. All the Cornish traffic had to pass through the city and there were constant queues of motor cars and horsedrawn vehicles throughout the town. The roads in fact were highly dangerous but we were trained in traffic consciousness from a very early age, and as I say, there was always a helpful constable around to assist the young, the old or the incapacitated.

Edgerton was quite a happy school I think. At any rate, I enjoyed my schooling there. It was run in an atmosphere of relaxed discipline with a strong accent on Christian principles. This entailed morning assemblies, several periods of religious instruction each week and regular attendance at the Cathedral for special Christian festivals. There was due regard paid to the conventions of the time, which the young will no doubt find highly diverting. For instance, the rule which decreed that gloves must always be worn with school uniform, and the one which forbade the eating of sweets in the streets. I am sure the Board of Equal Opportunities would be incensed to know that though in the summer term we played tennis for our own pleasure, cricket was taught to us to enable us to follow the game and trail around with our male relatives. Thank goodness we weren't made to play soccer or rugger on the same principle. Hockey was bad enough. That was played on a windswept pitch in Prince of Wales Road in the winter and as I couldn't run with pads on, I invariably ended up with earache and battered shins. What I liked was netball.

Our curriculum was much the same as in a boys' school, though with possibly a stronger accent on arts and less on mathematics and science. Indeed, our science lessons were hilarious, conducted as they were in the school boilerhouse. However, with the aid of a few Bunsen burners, some pipettes and flasks of various sizes, we learned about such things as volume and mass, about the properties of air and other gases, and the principles of osmosis. The conductivity of heat through metal was demonstrated by the simple expedient of placing a long poker in the firebox of the central heating boiler. Did I say central heating? It wasn't very effective, save in the kindergarten, and it was common for us to sit for hours in rooms so cold that the windows had frost patterns on them. By modern criteria, we should all have died of hypothermia. Though many of us suffered from chilblains however, I think we had fewer colds and infections than modern children, probably because we were made to walk and exercise more, and were sent to school warmly clad. Those were the days of Chilprufe vests, liberty bodices and fleecy-lined knickers.

The school was run by three sisters; Miss Gardiner the oldest was Headmistress. She was very dignified, with long dark skirts, and always wore a suitably subduing expression on her face. Miss Elsie was much jollier, indeed the most popular of the three. She was always arrayed in a gym slip and had a whistle perpetually swinging from her neck. The only time I saw her in a dress was on a Speech Day when I failed to recognise her. Miss Doreen was a Norland nurse with Froebel training. She had charge of the kindergarten and transition, for which duties a kind of nurse's outfit was deemed appropriate. With the aid of her part-time assistant, Miss Ralling, Miss Doreen coped with about fifty pupils who, when eight or nine years of age, could read, write, add up and subtract, who knew their tables up to twelve-times, and could do long division and subtraction and all sums in pounds, shillings and pence. They were then considered ready for the rigours of Form One, where English Grammar, French conversation and more formal instruction in History, Geography and Nature Study began. In the kindergarten we learned to read by the phonetic system, we imbibed spelling by rote and our tables by chanting. Able but lazy pupils were rewarded with dunce's caps while backward ones were encouraged by kindness and given extra help. Bad behaviour was rewarded by such horrific punishments as standing in the corner or being sent outside the door! These simple punishments worked well enough for most of us, but one boy posed a challenge to our mentors. He would distract the whole school with his roars of rage when outside the door and had the ability to wet himself when standing in the corner. He grew into a perfectly charming fellow - I met him years later at a cocktail party and had a near irresistible urge to remind him of our early school days together, but for once prudence triumphed over impulse!

Having recovered from their rage over the cricket, I think the Equal Opportunities Commission would have approved of the school curriculum. We were taught needlework in the lower school it's true, but not a duster or a saucepan was ever seen or mentioned. It was taken for granted that we learned the domestic arts at home, and school was the place for the mental disciplines. We were fortunate to be taught art by Miss Pitman. Primrose Pitman is the fine artist who etched practically all of pre-blitz Exeter. Many of her engravings were bought by the city archives department a few years ago, thus preserving a marvellous pictorial record of Exeter before the war.

Miss Rylance became our Principal after Miss Gardiner retired and this caused some consternation at the time because she was a Methodist and hitherto, the school had had an Anglican tradition. Quite a few pupils were withdrawn but those of us who remained became very fond of her and grew to appreciate her innate goodness. She was comparatively modern in outlook and actually arrived in a car, an old Austin, in which she drove from her home at Southport at a top speed, it was alleged, of no more than twenty-five miles an hour. I had a private theory that she decided to become a motorist because of her self-confessed habit of falling asleep on trains and missing her destinations. The arrival of Miss Rylance coincided with the Charleston at the peak of its popularity and we smaller fry formed the audience as older, more sophisticated pupils slung their girdles low over their hips and danced up and down the stone-floored cloakroom. This was a gay change from the solemn Greek routines we practised in our music and movement lessons. At home, our parents taught us to waltz and fox-trot in the kitchen passage to the strains of Victor Sylvester from our old HMV gramophone. What pleasure we derived from that old gramophone in the twenties. Radio was still in its infancy. Brother Bruce spent hours with contraptions of valves and cats' whiskers, trying to home in on transmissions from the old Savoy Hill. His efforts yielded faint, uncertain results but our old HMV never let us down and we acquired an extensive collection of records, ranging from the angelic renderings of 'Oh for the wings of a dove' by the choirboy Ernest Lough, through the classical repertoire to comic songs.

We walked everywhere until we were old enough to acquire bicycles. We were well situated in Alphington Road, close to the river where, with brother Bruce in charge, we canoed and hired rowing boats, and explored the delights of the canal basin; here were usually moored one or two coasters unloading timber or coal, gravel, cement or numerous other cargoes. It was a tidy, workmanlike place in those days, full of interesting smells from the fragrance of the piled timber to the metallic odour of the coal tips and the sharp smell emanating from the malt houses. Pinces Gardens, hidden away in Queens Road, was another favoured haunt. Here were tennis courts and a bowling green, beautifully tended flower borders and a yew-lined lawn, ideal for picnics and childish games, where we played under the strict eye of the peppery head gardener. The great glory of Pinces Gardens is an ancient wisteria archway, the length of a tennis court; I am glad to say it still flourishes.

As we got older, we went further afield on our bicycles or by train. We could travel from St Thomas Station in Cowick Street to the picturesque village of Ide for tuppence ha'penny return. In the blackberry season, one of the most fruitful fields adjoined the halt at Ide so we hadn't far to carry the picnic basket on arrival, or the blackberry harvest on our return. We knew where to find the earliest primroses, or the hedges of dog violets, white and mauve. I remember being invited inside the big gate to Perridge House, to watch the astonishing spectacle of thousands upon thousands of baby frogs emerging from the large pool there. Sometimes we 'scrumped' for fallen apples in the orchards now occupied by houses; we risked being chased by the red-faced farmer, but the station master was our friend; he would watch out for us and "halloo" loudly to tell us the return train was due.

We loved the coast, and in summer would cycle several times a week to Exmouth or Dawlish Warren, Freda travelling on Bruce's cycle rack and Marjory giving John a hefty shove to get him up the hills. We knew Exmouth well. Mother had a theory that we needed sea air after the ills and chills of winter, so she was wildly adventurous and at Eastertime, rented a so-called boathouse at the Point at Exmouth, near the busy little dock. Our favourite was called The Retreat, a converted boat's hull which occupied a plot of land surrounded by sea, from which a boat could be moored. Here every year we met up with our Butler family friends, and together we enjoyed complete freedom - we tore around without shoes, playing 'hares and hounds' or boating when the tide was right. It was too cold for swimming but we both paddled and shrimped and watched the ships entering and leaving the dock, or the helmeted divers working on the dock gates. It was a very busy little port and a source of never-ending interest. It is sad to think that it is now closed, to be replaced by a marina and tall apartment blocks.

On special days Father would take us further afield by car; to Dartmoor perhaps, or Bickleigh Bridge at nutting time, or to Ladram Bay at Otterton, where we would be affronted to find another picnic party.

Picnicking at Ladram, Otterton, 1922

In retrospect, those early years of childhood were a golden age for us. We led simple lives, bound by simple rules of behaviour, which included respect for our elders and for honesty and truthfulness, and consideration for others. Above all, we were brought up to be independent. Though lacking the modern trappings of the young, we were sometimes unhappy but never bored. We felt secure in the ambience of a properly regulated home and I think we were very fortunate.

Our Grandmother Reynolds sometimes accompanied us on holidays to Exmouth and no story of my young days would be complete without mention of her. She was petite and pretty, determined, lively and utterly feckless. When Grandfather Reynolds died - of worry Father used to say - no one seemed to know what happened to his estate. He came of the Reynolds family that produced the portrait painter, Sir Joshua, and was in fact his heir through an indirect line. Unfortunately, his considerable estate came to an Uncle, a sick man with an unscrupulous housekeeper who, by forging signatures, sold off most of his assets for practically nothing, to help her errant son out of the clutches of his gambling debtors. So there was, alas, no inheritance but even so, Grandfather must have had considerable assets of his own. The Reynolds family produced scholars and clerics and a line of horologists, one of whom had a London manufactory where he invented and patented the Reynolds clock movement which I gather was a great success. I suppose Grandfather descended from this branch and had a well-known watchmaking and jewellery business in Plymouth.

Grandmother Clara Reynolds was very extravagant and when short of money, would pawn her beautiful jewellery which her long-suffering husband would then have to redeem. My Father used to say that she had never seemed like a Mother and treated her six children with the utmost casualness. He was very fond of Clara's Mother, his granny Bennett, who was a very intelligent and refined old lady. He described taking tea with her. The maid Lizzy would bring in the tray with its silver teapot and kettle, and wait for granny to take the key from her chatelaine with which to open the beautiful tea caddy. She would mix the teas to her satisfaction, then let Lizzy pour on boiling water, and there would be saffron buns and cake to eat. Granny Bennett had very interesting tales to tell for she had led an extraordinary life. She had been brought up on a yacht in the Mediterranean. Her Father, Squire Stanbury, had been involved in a smuggling ring at Cawsand which comprised all the villagers and local dignitaries including the local vicar. After a fracas with Revenue officers, one man was unfortunately killed. Squire Stanbury escaped with his wife and daughter to his yacht and his estate was sequestrated by the Crown. He was never able to come to England again for fear of capture, but in time his wife and daughter returned to Plymouth after years of foreign wanderings and all kinds of adventures. I suppose Clara had some of her Grandfather's recklessness but she was a sore trial to her Mother, I gather. Grandfather Reynolds had possessed letters written by Samuel Johnson to Sir Joshua but they disappeared after his death. My Father said that Clara burnt them, like as not, not caring or realising their historical importance. She sold everything she could lay her hands on, spending the money like water, and ending up with nothing to finish her younger son's education.

Nothing daunted, she decided to take up nursing. We had a photograph of her in full nurse's rig, looking very fetching though lacking any qualifications I expect. When quite old, she came into a little money from some Canadian relatives and spent her days visiting her various children, creating terrible mischief amongst them all. As children we found her great fun. She would spend hours playing cards with us and telling us all sorts of extraordinary stories and smoking dreadful cigarettes called Dr Blozzer's Mentholated cigarettes. My Mother found her long visits very trying. I remember the night she made herself a hot toddy and poured boiling water into a beautiful crystal tumbler. Not surprisingly, it shattered and when Mother showed her dismay, Granny Clara exclaimed testily "My dear Nellie, what a fuss! What are you bothering about? It's only a glass!"

Next day she went to Woolworths and returned in triumph bearing two cheap Czechoslovakian glasses. "There you are my dear Nellie, two for the price of one!" she exclaimed brightly as she placed them on the table. "It is so silly to fuss about such trifles."

Grandmother Clarke was very different, quiet and dignified and conventional. She came from Brightlingsea in Essex. Her Father was a Roote and came from a line of sea captains, while her Mother was an Eagle who were shipowners and builders. I think their wedding caused some consternation as the shipowners thought themselves superior to the ships' captains. Mother told us that many of the Brightlingsea houses were filled with beautiful wood panelling taken from the broken-up vessels. I have often thought I would like to visit this small seaport but now I fear it is too late.

Grandfather Clarke, Volunteer Fireman, c. 1880

Grandfather Clarke was an engineer. He patented a device to prevent early steamships from blowing up at sea. No one took it up because it was expensive to fit but the year he ceased to pay the patent fee, an Act was passed in Parliament saying it must fitted to all steamships. He worked with William Morris, later Lord Nuffield, on various automobile projects and was the owner of the first motor car to come into east Kent. When Parliament repealed the law requiring a red flag to be carried in front of all motor cars, he immediately went to Germany and arranged to import German cars. We have a lovely photograph of my Mother in one of these early machines. It had tiller steering. She is wearing a motoring dress and a huge hat complete with veil. Grandfather became a partner in a large motoring business, Stevensons, in Tunbridge Wells. There were two fascinating characters in charge of the petrol pumps. One was called Campney - he had a cleft palate and was very difficult to understand but he was always very kind to us children - and the other one, Callow, was a communist. I hope I've got their names the right way round. "Come the revolution," Callow used to say, "the workers will take over this business and you'll be out, Mr Clarke. We'll be bosses then." After years and years of saving, he bought his own little house and was furious when grandpa told him he had joined the ranks of the capitalists!

We used to love inspecting all the beautiful new cars in the showrooms, the new Morrises and Wolseleys, Austins and stately Daimlers and Bentleys, all polished to mirror brightness. Sometimes Uncle Hal or Uncle Frank, my Mother's brothers who were also in the business, would take us for drives in these splendid machines and that was a great excitement. Our summer trips to Tunbridge Wells were full of interest and we enjoyed meeting all our cousins. We were parcelled out amongst the various relations for although my grandparents had a large house in Prospect Road, our high spirits would have been too much for them.

Chapter 2 - Growing Up in the Thirties

We were fast growing up as the twenties passed into the thirties. Brother Bruce reached his eighteenth birthday and then Father gave him his Wolseley car which had given yeoman service for many years. Father had used it for business and it had been on umpteen trips from Devonshire to Kent, a ten-hour journey in those days. One of my Kentish cousins still remembers a journey from Tunbridge Wells to Exeter. Eric shared the dickey seat with younger brother John and me while baby Freda sat wedged between Father and Mother in the front. Half way to Exeter, it started to rain and we all took shelter for a while, then when it abated we were tucked up with rugs and set off again. Once more the heavens opened and in despair at the thought of not reaching home until after dark, my parents decided to press on and we three occupants of the open dickey sat on the floor so that the lid could be three-quarters lowered to keep us dry. Eric is an amusing chap and to this day, we still have hysterics when we recall that trip, squatting on the floor in near darkness with just enough air to breathe and water trickling down our necks. Bruce painted the Wolseley bright yellow and we called it the 'Yellow Peril', in which we had numerous experiences!

Homeward Bound from Tunbridge Wells in the old Wolseley, 1929

Motoring, although becoming more comfortable, was still quite adventurous in those days. For instance, we had a rather hair-raising experience when Marjory and I were staying in Sussex with Uncle Frank and his wife Madge. Uncle took us for a spin in his Bentley. Being unused to children, he allowed Marjory to sit in the front seat with me on her knee. In the excitement of rounding a bend at speed, I put my elbow on the door catch. The door flew open, Uncle slammed on his brakes and I flew out of the door. But for Marjory's presence of mind in grabbing my ankles, I would have fallen right into the village duckpond. Poor Uncle was shattered and to our great disappointment, although we promised not to tell Mother, he drove with great caution after that. I spent many holidays in Wadhurst with Uncle Frank and Auntie Madge. She was a famed cook and I was possessed of a cast-iron digestion. My brothers and sisters, with the brutal frankness of such kin, vowed I was only invited so often because I could enjoy her rich and delicious food without being sick. They were very kind and arranged all sorts of treats. For a week or two it was marvellous but longer visits tended to drag and I missed the family.

Indeed, one feature of my Sussex visits I didn't enjoy at all - Sunday luncheon with my Aunt's Mother who was the matriarch of a large family. Her house was big and dark and stuffed with furniture and knick-knacks in the Victorian style which still lingered on into the thirties. The luncheon was equally stiff and formal and served by a great butler who made me hiccup into my soup one day when he suddenly caught my eye and gave me a wink. He was obviously rather sorry for the little girl marooned in this sea of grown-ups. I looked for his winks on future visits and he usually managed one or two. There was also an ancient parrot who not only spoke but actually swore in French, and a most exciting loo framed in polished mahogany. The pan was of china, decorated with a picture of Windsor Castle and when you pulled the lever, the bottom of the Castle fell out and allowed the cascading water to gurgle away.

One day Uncle Frank took me to see the fragile aeroplane in which Captain Bleriot first crossed the Channel and on another more tragic occasion, we all saw the burnt-out shell of an Imperial Airways aircraft which had crashed near Croydon killing most of the passengers and crew. What a contrast to Captain Bleriot's plane! It really showed the tremendous development of aircraft over a comparatively few years.

When I returned home and told the family of these events, my stories were capped by Marjory and Bruce. They had been holidaying in Basingstoke with Auntie Con and Uncle Tufty and were taken to see the Schneider Air Cup Race. These races were a great feature of the aviation year and all the famous aces from all over the world came and took part, and I think they must have been very thrilling to watch. If the twenties consolidated the age of the motor car, the thirties saw the great development of travel by air, and to our generation it was all tremendously exciting. For Freda and me the supreme thrill came a few years later when a pilot friend of Father's took us up in a tiny open plane belonging to Sir Alan Cobham's Flying Circus. Flying in a modern aeroplane is very dull in comparison.

Fashionwise, the thirties were dreary. The style and zing of the 'roaring twenties' had evaporated and apart from evening wear which still had great elegance, the most memorable items of apparel were the Oxford Bags and plus-fours of menfolk, and the quite extraordinary hats of the women. Marjory had her fair share of strange headgear which all caused us great hilarity.

As the thirties progressed, domestic help became far more difficult to obtain. We no longer had a resident maid and Mother relied on a series of 'dailies'. Sadly Mrs Mainford had to retire due to her rapidly worsening rheumatism and this was a great blow. She was an integral part of the family and to Mother, more friend and confidante than servant. I really think that her departure finally convinced Mother that she no longer could cope with a three-storey house with four flights of stairs and she began to search for her dream house. A commodious one it would have to be but on two floors only and with a garage and certainly a garden. A three-year search was started but nothing came to light. Meanwhile life went on at Trevone and Marjory and I had to undertake little light duties at weekends. One of us had to dust the drawing-room and the dining-room while the other did the weekend shopping locally. All of us, including the boys, had to share the washing-up. Mother, as I have said, was quite progressive in her ideas and the boys were even taught the rudiments of cooking.

Alphington Street wasn't terribly attractive but we were all fond of the tradespeople and we would set out quite happily with Pru carrying the shopping basket. She knew the shopkeepers as well as we did and went on ahead, quickly popping in and out of the shops where she knew she was likely to be given a sweet. Ralph Warre and his widowed Mother ran the small greengrocery while the buxom Misses Badcock looked after the dairy of that name and made the most delicious ice cream out of the previous day's leftover clotted cream. Thick yellow crusted cream was piled in large shallow copper pans and displayed in the window with hand-turned Devonshire butter, and there were china hens filled with eggs. One of the sisters delivered the milk and was one of the first traders in the street to give up her pony for a van. Our milk was delivered by young Mr Clark whose pony knew exactly at which house to stop. His widowed Mother was the boss and ran the little dairy shop. Our bread came from Hardings, another family concern like Baileys the shoemakers, where Mr Bailey cobbled while his pretty wife sold the shoes. Port House Laundry was run by two sisters who I think lived in the house which fronted onto Alphington Street while the laundry was at the back. A bad-tempered parlourmaid used to answer the door when we took Father's stiff collars to be laundered. It was from Osbornes, the stationery shop, that we got our newspapers and all our pencils, crayons and paints, while haberdashery, hats and general goods such as ribbons were available at Courtenays Corner Shop, also run by a woman. At Lethbridges, the high-class poulterers in Cowick Street, three sons worked in the busy shop while their handsome Mother sat in the cashier's box controlling everything.

Several of the larger shops in the city were owned and run by women and I can think of at least two female pharmacists. It was difficult for me to think of pre-war women as oppressed and downtrodden, except for a few perhaps who were unlucky enough to have drunken brutes for husbands. In the majority of working-class homes, the husbands handed over their wage packets every week and were given back a little beer and 'baccy money.

Gradually more and more women were taking up careers. Teaching, secretarial work and nursing were traditional spheres and indeed, I suppose the most influential posts were those of hospital Matrons who wielded tremendous power, not only over patients and nurses but over the doctors as well, and also the trustees and governors. I suppose the professions were the hardest nuts to crack but two daughters of Ernest Crosse, our family solicitor, became solicitors in the early thirties and the other one qualified after the war. Several women followed Dr Mabel Gates, a medical practitioner in the city, and I can think of one or two architects, but still not many girls thought seriously about careers. The first object was to find a suitable husband and raise a family.

Mother was rather ahead of her time I think. She was determined that each of her daughters should have some sort of training. "You may not marry," she used to say, "or you may be widowed, and none of my daughters is going to end up as a companion to some old tabby cat." She was determined on domestic science for me. "But Mummy, I want to be a journalist," I protested. "Girls don't go in for journalism," she said. Well, when visiting Auntie Madge and Uncle Frank, I often met Mr Murray who managed the family firm that brought out the Kent & Sussex Courier. "I could write and ask Mr Murray how to set about it," I suggested, but Mother had made up her mind. "You can't possibly bother him," she said. "It might cost a lot of money and you would need to pay for your keep while you were training. It might be years. Oh no, it wouldn't do at all." And so I was enrolled at Maynard School for the domestic science course which, when I became used to it, was really very interesting, particularly the study of dietetics and the science of food. We were also instructed in housewifery, cookery and laundry work, pattern making and dress making, French, English, Biology and also a craft of our choice. The pattern making I found complicated. My brother John actually showed me how to put the pieces together to make a pair of knickers!

Brothers are very nice to have, and can be very helpful. My brother Bruce, for instance, explained the facts of life to me when I went to him in disgust after hearing what I thought were depraved and dirty stories of love-making. He was wonderful and made it all sound so beautiful that I never worried about it again. I think I was about thirteen years old at the time. Boys were taught these things at school. Plain facts in their Biology classes and the spiritual and loving side of sex was explained by the school chaplain. This seems to be an admirable way of tackling sex education which sadly was not provided in the average girls' school.

However, I digress. My year at Maynards went very quickly and I made some good friends who have remained so after nearly sixty years. Most of us had already obtained our School Certificates and we took Parts 1 and 2 together, so the two-year course only took one year.

For practical experience, Joyce Rogers and I enrolled on a course of Institutional Management at the Royal Devon & Exeter Hospital in Southernhay, Exeter. The Hospital had been started in 1743 by the young Dean Clarke. People are inclined to think that free healthcare didn't arrive until after the last war but in fact, most cities had a general hospital and these were built very largely by charitable donations. No one was ever refused entry at the R.D. & E. In emergencies, extra beds were pushed into the wards and even placed in the circulation areas outside. When patients were fit to be questioned, the hospital almoner would discuss their financial situations and they paid nothing or perhaps a shilling a week if very poor, or the full cost if they were sufficiently well off. There were private rooms which brought in useful extra money and for which quite a high charge was made. There were few administrators - a hospital secretary, a treasurer, an almoner, a housekeeper, a supplies officer. They all had their own secretaries and there were a few clerks. Matron of course had an assistant and her own secretary. She was the hospital powerhouse, helped by a hard-working board of governors. There were about two hundred and fifty beds and all the sisters, nurses and domestic staff were resident, so altogether I think we catered for about five hundred people with just thirteen staff in the kitchens. The kitchens had already been re-sited on the top floor which prevented cookery smells pervading the building, and was also considered safer in case of fire. The Sister in Charge had been on a special course to St Thomas's Hospital and she returned to our kitchens with all the latest ideas on equipment. There were steaming cabinets and cupboards, hot cupboards, soup boilers, a large fish and chip fryer, electric bacon slicer, three enormous refrigerating chambers and a modern Hobart mixer and mincing machine.

There were different grades of meals - Domestics and Patients, and Nurses, Sisters, Doctors and Matron. The doctors all gave their services free and newly graduated doctors spent a year working full-time, day and night, for nothing but their keep, and so it was felt essential to feed them well. Each week the various meals were costed. This Joyce and I sometimes had to do. I can recall a week when the patients were fed for 5/11d each. Much food was donated and at harvest time, when Joyce and I started working, all the produce from the churches came to the hospital. Thousands of eggs were pickled in isinglass, thousands of pounds of jams and chutneys were made, masses of onions and cabbages were pickled and mounds of apples were stored for future use. Not a penny was wasted in that establishment. If one broke a cup or a bedpan, whatever, the pieces had to be kept and then we all had to wait for 'open stores' day on Wednesday when the Supplies Sister gave us a wigging, asked us how we had broken the thing, gave us a replacement and told us she didn't expect to see us again. Not surprisingly, she very rarely did.

After a few weeks in the main kitchen, I started working in the diet kitchen under the very competent head cook and Joyce was in the meat and dairy kitchen with Mabel, the second cook; Sister Kitchen was in overall control. We worked a forty-eight hour week including a Sunday turn, and in return for our free help, we received free meals and a very special privilege of a coffee tray every morning! After a few months, the head cook was due for her annual month's holiday and the thrifty governors, having received a satisfactory report from 'Sister Kitchen', asked me to take charge of the diet kitchen in her place. Despite the fact that there was a very nice young assistant cook, I was scared stiff at the thought of the responsibility: it meant arranging the diet sheets and the dessert menus and controlling the staff, as well as the actual food production, but I found it quite exhilarating and after surviving the first few days, I found it was the most wonderful experience.

By the end of that year, 1937, the family were installed in a new family home in Lower Hill Barton Road. It was a most convenient house with all mod cons and fulfilled Mother's dream of a house on two floors. It was very well built, although it only took four months. So well built in fact that it survived a thousand pound bomb in the garden during the war which sent a great lump of subsoil bouncing through the roof. Apart from an enormous hole in the tiles, the house was perfectly all right, and not a window broken, though the shock waves created much damage round about.

After finishing our time at the hospital, Joyce and I were given certificates by Matron and then I spent a year doing jobs at various hospitals and establishments around the city; but I still worked for free in return for experience and I was beginning to feel that I would like to have a job which actually paid me some money! I wanted to travel, to learn to fly; the future seemed full of promise, life was marvellous and I just wanted to get on with it!

Chapter 3 - Work at The Fisherman's Cot at Bickleigh Bridge

I applied for several posts, then a third letter of rejection popped through the Trelake letter box one fine June morning in 1939. "Good credentials, but too young," it conveyed in essence. "Apply again in five years' time." Five years! Why by then I'd be four-and twenty, and I didn't relish the prospect of living at home for ever and a day, on pocket money of half-a-crown a week! After two years' training in domestic science and institutional management and a further year spent as an unpaid stop-gap working in local hospitals for experience, 'twas high time I felt for gainful employment.

And the parents deserved a break, after bringing up six children in the difficult days of the Great War and the equally fraught ones which followed. Molly and Bruce, my elders, had already fled the nest and Marjory, the next in seniority, was usefully employed as Father's right-hand woman. That left me, the first of the post-war brood, my younger brother John still at Exeter School, and baby sister Freda who trudged from Lower Hill Barton Road to Edgerton School in Pennsylvania.

It was useless, it seemed, applying for jobs by answering press advertisements; a different strategy was needed - but what? As I pondered on the doorstep, Father passed me, en route to the garage. Despite severe gassing in the Great War and the harassment of six children, he was still, I thought, remarkably slim and youthful. "Another rejection?" he enquired quizzically. "Well never mind old girl - keep your chin up!" That was his usual cliché in times of stress. In fact, we were brought up on exhortations of "keep your chin up!" and "don't lose your head!" and I found neither of much use just then. But inspiration was at hand - a neighbour came to the gate at that moment in search of Mother. "No luck at the Domestic Registry!" she called out tragically, "and Mary is leaving this week!"

Domestic Registry! Why hadn't I thought of that? Bless Mrs Fairchild! I got to the car as Father was about to take off and begged a lift into Exeter. He dropped me off in High Street and I made my way to the hitherto unconsidered Domestic Registry.

I had no idea what to expect as I climbed the lino-covered stairs and knocked on a chipped brown door. I was bidden to enter by a small woman who sat behind a large desk. She besought me to be seated. She had a very white face and very black hair and large black-rimmed spectacles. The effect was somewhat ghostly.

Despite a strange accent - best described, I think, as mangled Oxford with muddled h'aspirates - she proved very business-like. "There is a post for a cook at the Fisherman's Cot," she said, then added doubtfully that she didn't know if a lady would suit. (How dated this sounds now!) I replied rather huffily that I didn't want a position as a cook anyway; a Caterer or Institutional Housekeeper perhaps - but already she had rung the Cot and was making an appointment for the following afternoon. A 'lady' it seemed would be acceptable - there were already "two h'others on the staff, and the h'Exmoor h'air's so 'ealthy, don't you faind?" "Oh yes," I agreed, "and the Fisherman's Cot is a charming place, but I don't want a job as a cook!"

Even now, after nigh on sixty years, I can still visualise her as she looked me straight in the eye and waggled an admonitory finger. "Now look 'ere, Miss Reynolds," she said, her voice coming off its high horse. "You take my h'advice - if you're offered this job, you take it! You've got some useful bits o' paper an' no mistake, but it's getting begun that counts you know - for until you've got begun, you can't get nowhere!"

I couldn't fault her logic and neither could the parents; though somewhat disapproving, they agreed the appointment should be honoured, and next day Father drove me out to the Cot at Bickleigh Bridge.

It was - and still is - a delightful place. The timbered building - now much altered - snuggled beneath its thatch on the bank below the waterfall which sang and shimmered and frothed in the summer sunshine. There's no more picturesque spot in England, I daresay, and it has always been a favourite family haunt.

Father was bowled over by the manageress, Mrs Harding. She was the personification of charm and good humour; she must have been ravishing when young, I thought, with her huge grey eyes and blue-black hair only just beginning to lose its lustre.

After perusing my C.V., she suggested I might undertake the catering as well as the cooking, which would make a more interesting job. The kitchen was bright and well-equipped (not least with a kitchen porter!!) and enjoyed a fine view of the river; the proposed bedroom, though minute, was also bright and sunny - but best of all was the salary - £8 per month "all found"! Undreamed-of riches! I took 'Black-eyed Susan's' h'advice. I accepted the post with alacrity and got myself 'begun'.

At the Fisherman's Cot time flew. Life was so hectic that at the day's end I flopped into bed, dead-beat; but at least it wasn't boring! After the first few days, Mrs Harding left me to cope alone with the help of the inestimable K.P. Walters.

The hotel boasted few bedrooms - about seven I think, at that time, but its charming situation attracted much passing trade. We averaged fifty-six lunches a day, and innumerable teas and coffees and dinners.

I planned the menus and 'phoned the orders in between frying eggs and grilling fish for breakfast, while Walters rinded bacon or prepared the vegetables for lunch. The beverages, the cereals and toast were served from the still room by a dear little Devonshire dumpling called Mrs Cooper. Her son, Tom, was the local milkman, and was possessed of the bluest eyes, the ruddiest cheeks and the widest grin I have ever seen on anyone! He had also inherited his Mother's genial disposition, and the pair of them lived happily in a run-down thatched cottage - since beautifully restored - which sits on the corner of Cadeleigh Hill where it joins the lane to the Castle.

The rest of the staff consisted of the other 'ladies' - two sisters called Stackpoole. One had charge of the bedrooms and relieved Mrs Harding in Reception, while the other ran the busy dining room with the help of a waitress called Mabel.

The sisters had evolved an interesting life style; they had inherited the family home from their mill-owning Father, but without sufficient money to run it. Having no marketable skills save domestic ones, they spent hard-working summers in English hotels and luxurious winters as guests in Swiss ones!

They were extremely efficient, and pleasant enough - but apart from work we had little in common, and never shared off-duty activities. They made beds and laid dining tables while I cooked non-stop. Lunchtime was always hectic, and the fare, though not fanciful, was all prepared from the best ingredients in English country house style. There were usually two roasts, and a couple of other main courses, with roast and steamed potatoes and two or three vegetables. There was _always_ a milk pudding, a cold sweet and assorted fruit tarts, all served with lashings of Devonshire cream. Dinner was a five-course meal, consisting of home-made soup or hors d'œuvres, a fish course followed by meat or game with all the trimmings, desserts and savouries. There were also the scones and cakes to be prepared for the numerous afternoon teas.

Life was busy, and free time precious. I usually spent it exploring the countryside on foot, or taking riding lessons with a great local character named Stooke-Hallett. On days off I went home, courtesy of the "Tivvy Bumper" which stopped across the bridge at Cadeleigh Halt.

In retrospect, that summer of '39 seems for ever sunny; the garden at home was perfumed and gay with clove pinks and roses and great mauve cushions of cat-mint, the young trees in the orchard were heavy with fruit, and the kitchen garden hummed with bees - Mother's bees. She talked of keeping chickens as well; despite the Munich Agreement of '38, there was much talk of war. Mother was a realist; she remembered the terrible food shortages of the '14 - '18 War, and as her finely-tuned maternal antennae warned of the coming danger to her beloved sons, I think it helped her to think on practical matters.

Family and friends had strong reason to bless her prescience in the years ahead, but while life continued normally, Mother's "bees and birds" were a bit of a joke!

I always enjoyed the rail journey from Cadeleigh to Exeter and back; the old Exe Valley line was a delight with its little neat stations a riot of vivid annuals, its station masters/cum porters so helpful, and the country passengers so full of cheerful chatter. A very stout party had us in fits of laughter one day; her farmer husband had lately invested in a tractor "and he gets proper aeriated" she confided, "when he calls out 'whoa' an' the darned thing takes no notice!" All agreed 'twould be a sad day "when all the hosses be replaced by they noisy contraptions." Another day, I remember, a consignment of top hats at Bramford Speke caused much conjecture - "who was gettin' wed then?" or "maybe they was for Ascot?" "Ascot be over!" said a plump matron dismissively so the wedding notion prevailed for the rest of the journey.

One morning I feared I would miss the train from Exeter; I puffed aboard just in time, and the guard was about to blow his whistle when a passenger called out in urgent tones, "we can't go yet, George isn't here!" So we waited for George who strolled on several minutes later.

The old G.W.R. was unbeatable for service!

Chapter 4 - Clouds of War

There was excellent trout and salmon fishing at the Fisherman's Cot, so, naturally, the larger proportion of visitors were fly fishermen - often accompanied by long-suffering wives - but sometimes we entertained country lovers in search of peace and tranquillity.

One such was a lady novelist called Mrs Welsh, with whom I struck up a friendship. Under Mrs Harding's benign rule there was no demarcation between staff and guests, and one afternoon we walked together along the leafy lanes to Bickleigh Castle. With its mediaeval keep and lily-filled moat, it has a fairy-tale quality, and it reminded my companion of Rhineland castles she had seen. She had travelled extensively and kept me entertained until we arrived back at the Cot.

A figure in air force blue was silhouetted on the dining room verandah, "a Greek God come to life!" exclaimed Mrs Welsh (who was of a romantic disposition) but, "it's my brother!" I exclaimed and rushed to greet Bruce.

He had a short leave it seemed, and had arrived home the previous day. Mrs Harding, ever thoughtful, sent Mabel with a tray of tea, and we spent a happy hour sitting on my favourite grassy knoll by the waterfall. He spoke lyrically of the joys of flying (now that he had a decent "crate") and we laughed anew at his reminiscences of the preliminary flying training school; the Air Force was so short of planes that the raw recruits received their early instruction on old bi-planes of duodetic construction; their first task was to learn to patch the canvas wings!

It wasn't funny really - Germany had created a formidable Air Force. She had been re-arming for years and her intentions were strictly dishonourable. Hitler had warned the world in "Mein Kampf." But no one had taken any notice.

Bruce became, suddenly, deadly serious. "There's going to be war you know," he said quietly. I can still recall the quiver of fear that shot through me as I looked at him; it was as though I saw him for the first time. He did look rather like a Greek God with his finely chiselled features and penetrating grey-blue eyes. "Do you really think it will happen Bruce?" The fear turned into a little frisson of excitement, then back to fear again as he replied, "it's inevitable, our training has been speeded up. Hitler and his gang are unspeakable and they're doing unspeakable things! Just imagine the Nazis ruling the world!" 'Heavens, imagine the horror of it - we'd all been living in Cloud Cuckoo Land - hadn't Mr Chamberlain settled it all at Munich?' we'd told each other as we stocked up with food and bought Anderson air-raid shelters as a sort of insurance policy. But in reality Mr Chamberlain had not made a peace, he'd merely bought a little time, a little precious time and precious little of it. "And to think," said my brother, "that once I actually admired Hitler! I really thought he would be good for Germany - until I read Mein Kampf! That was an eye-opener! And then the Jewish Pogroms - oh, we hear all kinds of things, not a tenth of it gets into the papers, the Press is just full of wishful thinking!" His voice was full of an unusual passion, and there was a steely look in his eyes which sent a shiver of apprehension down my spine. "Bruce," I said, "do you really think it will happen?" He was quickly his old self again as he made ready to depart. "You 'eard!" he exclaimed in picturesque Air Force slang, "you ain't got cloth ears wot button up!" Over the space of fifty years, the memory of that afternoon remains as fresh as dew; it marked the end of a protracted pre-war adolescence. Nothing was ever quite the same again, though peace endured for a few weeks yet.

Life went on everywhere as usual, and though there was a feeling of unease abroad, few people changed their normal habits. At the Fisherman's Cot we served innumerable coffees, luncheons and teas to touring holiday-makers, as well as caring for our own guests. We were rushed off our feet; my day began at 7.00 am when before breakfast I made cakes and scones for the afternoon teas; we were lucky to be finished by 9.00 pm, but even so, with the energy of youth I nearly always took an 'unwinding' stroll along the riverside before going to bed.

I had an enchanting encounter with a salmon poacher on one of these nocturnal expeditions. I nearly fell over him, as he lay in a large clump of cow parsley by the water's edge. "Shush," he hissed and I was astounded to see a large salmon in the water, quite motionless, half cradled in one of his arms! The fish seemed mesmerised as he stroked it gently under its stomach. I stood utterly absorbed until suddenly the spell was broken with a splash; the poacher jerked his arm and sent his quarry spinning through the air in a glistening arc which landed at my feet.

"Hmm!" I murmured accusingly as I watched him gaff the beautiful thing and stuff it into a canvas bag. "Taking by tickling! My boss would not be at all amused!" "Don't let on," he coaxed, "my boss has promised me a fiver! He hasn't had any luck so far despite all his fancy gear!" I had thought the man looked familiar, and realised he was chauffeur to an American guest who had arrived a few days earlier in a Rolls Royce crammed with sporting gear and expensive leather luggage. "Do be quiet

Miss," he whispered fiercely as I started to laugh. "I've got five children to support - I daresn't get caught!"

Next day, by chance I happened to pass the yard where the fishermen were appraising their respective catches, when the Yank put his trophy on the scales. It proved to be the heaviest, and he was happily admiring it when one of the other fishermen came forward and peered at it suspiciously. Quick as a wink, the American whisked it off the scales and advanced on me. "With my compliments ma'am," he drawled as he thrust it into my arms. "We're off to London after lunch and my fish won't keep so good in this heat!" Though I applauded his quick thinking, I felt a blush reddening my cheeks, and could have murdered the grinning chauffeur lolling by the Rolls as I beat a guilty retreat with my trophy.

A few days later we were all grinning on the other side of our faces, when the news came of the combined Russo/German invasion of Poland. This was the crunch because of our Treaty of Friendship with Poland; Britain and France announced full mobilisation on September 1st, and next day began the great exodus of children from London and the great cities. The issue of gas masks was speeded up.

What sinister looking things they are! I have often wondered who had the imagination to design children's masks in the form of animal faces which turned the frightening horrors into objects of amusement. A surprisingly human touch amid the trauma of the times, on a par with the kindly Bishop who mingled with a crowd of confused evacuee children milling around Paddington Station. "I don't know where we're going, do you?" he had enquired of a lively bunch. "Why don't you ask the engine driver, sir? He ought'a know!" was their intelligent advice.

During the night of September 2nd I had an embarrassing encounter with the Misses Stackpoole; I couldn't sleep and arose to investigate when I heard muffled thumping noises coming from the stairway. The two sisters were creeping out with their baggage and confessed they were leaving; they'd left a note for Mrs Harding they said, and would I take the morning teas?

I think they were afraid their house might be requisitioned in their absence, but I was surprised by their lack of manners in leaving without notice or proper goodbyes. This experience was one of my first glimpses of human nature under stress, for the Misses Stackpoole were normally models of rectitude.

Next morning at 11.00 am Mr Chamberlain announced - rather as if it were a cricket match - that war with Germany would start at 5.00 pm. Guests and staff were all assembled in the sitting room to listen to the historic declaration on the radio. Although fully expected, the news nevertheless stunned us all. For a few moments there was a deathly hush; then an outburst of chatter followed by frantic activity.

All the guests trooped noisily upstairs to pack; then, apparently deciding with one mind that they might as well make the most of what might well be their last holiday for years, they all trooped down again. They would be staying on, they said. So we were left with a houseful of guests and practically no staff. But suddenly it didn't seem to matter very much. The whole tenor of life changed within minutes. We were all as one against the common foe. There was tremendous esprit I remember, the men helping Mabel to carry dishes, their wives volunteering to wash up.

Life acquired a surreal quality; no one knew what to expect next; we were in unknown territory, with only the radio to guide us.

The very first task was to tackle the black-out, and we raided the linen cupboard for spare blankets and bedspreads to pin across the windows 'ere night fell.

By next morning, Mrs Harding had new staffing arrangements in place. I seemed to have become her second-in-command. Mrs Cooper joyfully undertook the bedroom work and Mabel was able to show her capabilities now that the shadow of the awesome sisters was removed. Mrs Woodgates, the Proprietor's wife, arrived with great bales of the hideous 'black-out' material which had recently made its appearance on drapers' shelves. It took days to make all the necessary curtains, Mrs Woodgates, myself and Mrs Harding spending every spare minute at the sewing machine. The dining room in particular presented a mammoth task, as it had huge windows overlooking the waterfall. It was a beautiful room and would look hideous, I felt, draped in the funereal black. The result fulfilled my grimmest expectations.

Our nice young bobby bicycled all round his beat, warning everyone about the black-out regulations, which were to be vigorously enforced with fines, and imprisonment for persistent offenders! It was difficult at first to remember to switch off all the lights before opening outside doors, and to pull all the dark curtains before nightfall. It was always a trial, but eventually, as with so many uncomfortable things, we became accustomed to the eerie routine.

Apart from an exploratory raid on London, and the immediate despatch of a British Expeditionary Force to France - which included Lieutenant Kerry Harding, and several friends and relations - nothing much happened on land.

At sea, however, hostilities broke out within hours. The German Navy was well prepared with 'U' boats already in position in the shipping lanes. An early victim was the unmarked liner "Athenia", which had hundreds of children aboard bound for safety in America. This was a terrible war crime, and aroused even greater hostility towards the enemy.

By mid-October we'd suffered two further blows. Somehow a 'U' boat penetrated our defences at Scapa Flow and sank the battleship "Royal Oak" with nearly all hands - then Warsaw capitulated to the combined onslaught of the German and Russian invaders. As they proceeded to parcel up poor doomed Poland between them, our raison d'être for war with Germany disappeared; we were powerless to help our ally; but no one doubted that the conflict would continue, for the thought of the Nazis conquering Europe, and eventually dominating the entire world, was too awful to contemplate.

Although Hitler had revealed his thoughts and plans quite clearly in "Mein Kampf" a few years earlier, no one had taken him seriously, but now no one doubted his intentions and there were daily accounts of fresh iniquities committed by the Nazis.

How gullible we'd been! How amazingly complacent! All through the thirties when the Fuehrer ranted and re-armed in Germany, in England, people in high places who should have known better had accused Churchill of war-mongering when he tried to set the alarm-bells ringing. Now our chickens were coming home to roost.

Meanwhile, in our unimportant little patch of England, we had a small excitement one day when a platoon of soldiers arrived out of the blue and took possession of our car park. They slept in the garages and drilled and ate and carried out their ablutions on the forecourt. They'd come to guard the bridge against possible paratroopers; all the populace shared a manic fear of that modern martial phenomenon, and lived in daily dread of airborne invasion - which in fact never came about.

The Guardians of Bickleigh Bridge, 1939

We enjoyed playing host to the army - it made us feel important and involved in the great struggle. We loved their cheery whistling, their willing help with heavy parcels from the bus, their invitations to partake of tea, so strong and sweet a mouse could trot across it. One day the sergeant organised a drill display to amuse Angela Harding's grandchildren, when Daphne, their Mother, brought them out from Exeter to see the "soldiers like Daddy." We were bereft when they departed as suddenly as they had arrived.

By now all the holiday-makers had departed, and we were left with a few long stayers, including a dear old schoolmaster we nicknamed Mr Chips, who some years previously had retired to fish and garden at the Cot. Mrs Welsh stayed on awhile, and also the wife of a Brigadier who kept disappearing on strange missions abroad. An elderly couple who sought shelter from the perils of Bournemouth completed the guest list. Mrs Welsh wrote, the Brigadier's wife read novels or manicured her nails, Mr Chips "Dug for Victory" and the elderly Smiths took care of their health. It fascinated me to watch the self-centred old couple enter the dining room each morning armed with Bemax and Marmite, ready to discuss their ailments with anyone prepared to listen, oblivious it seemed to the great drama unfolding beyond our shores.

I subdued a feeling of restlessness by indulging in an orgy of food preservation. Fortunately Mrs Harding had laid in supplies of sugar, and the products of a bountiful harvest were jammed and pickled and chutnied, till the shelves of the store-cupboard positively groaned with glistening rows of jars and bottles. She also produced a splendid recipe for pickling pears in cider, and these became quite a hit for special occasions. Rationing was already severe with sugar, fats and meat in short supply, so my bottled fruits and relishes were a useful addition to the weekly menus.

The black-out was always a great trial; it was positively spooky in the open after dark, particularly when all the signposts had been removed. This was planned to confound incipient enemies, but in fact caused havoc amongst the indigenous population! At night, streams of confused and irritable travellers rang the front door bell praying for guidance and cursing the powers-that-be.

By December, there was still no action in France. There were terrific sea battles as the Germans sought to blockade the British Isles, but still all was eerily quiet on the Western Front. This was the period of the so-called "Phoney War". Mrs Cooper said she wished "they would get on and get it over with - it's like dressin' in black for a funeral and finding the corpse gone missing!"

There was certainly a great feeling of anti-climax after the first few hectic weeks of adjustment to wartime living. No parachutists fluttered from the skies, there were no battles in France and only sporadic air-raids in London. Many of the homesick children, so frantically evacuated from the cities, went back to their homes.

By Christmas the weather had turned bitterly cold; brother Bruce was snowbound in Scotland, and shortly afterwards we were snowbound in Devon. The snow turned to ice, and the waterfall below Bickleigh Bridge was frozen right across. For the first time in living memory it was possible - though perilous - to cross it from bank to bank. The roads were impassable for several days, and we lived in a sort of breathless hush, temporarily excluded from the outside world and its terrors.

During the freeze-up, a prisoner escaped from Dartmoor, and once more a guard was mounted on the bridge, this time by the police whose job it was to inspect the passengers in every passing car. Local bobbies and Special Constables from all the surrounding villages were drafted in pairs for round-the-clock surveillance - a terrible assignment in that appalling weather. We provided them with hot drinks by day, and at night left a pan of hot soup on the Aga for which they were truly grateful.

It was very interesting to talk to these guardians of the law, kindly men for the most part, but steady and authoritative, respected representatives of that vanished breed who policed rural England before the age of the permissive society, the hooligan and the lager lout. Our Bickleigh copper told us that he got more kudos for overseeing a peaceable community than for making a lot of arrests.

After a few days the escapee was found frozen to death on the moor; a small local tragedy while beyond our shores enormous ones were being enacted. Losses at sea were horrific - from aerial bombardment, from magnetic mines, from the deadly 'U' boat wolf packs which harried our convoys like foxes in a chicken-run.

The struggle sent shock waves throughout the country, and touched us at the Fisherman's Cot when Mabel received a fateful telegram. Her brother, a merchant seaman, was 'missing at sea', presumed drowned after his ship had been torpedoed. She was in a state of profound shock for weeks, carrying out her duties like an automaton and scarcely ever speaking.

It was some consolation to remember that our own H.M.S. Exeter had helped Ajax and Achilles to harry the great German battleship Graf Spee until, damaged, she slunk into Montevideo and scuttled herself. One less fox in the chicken-run!

Then, as the bitter winter gave way to a glorious spring, we rejoiced again at the capture of the German prison ship Altmark, and the consequent release of nearly three hundred allied prisoners.

In France, still the Nazis made no move. We were lulled into a sense of false security by the precociously warm weather which carpeted the river bank in a golden haze of daffodils. There was a record salmon run, I remember, so many fish that the waterfall was whipped into a creamy lather by the leaping beauties, creating a spectacle which brought sightseers from miles around.

As I surveyed the scene one afternoon, I was entertained by a young actor who was 'resting' at the Cot. He had an ambition to be a great Shakespearian actor, but I felt he was barking up the wrong tree for he had a natural talent to amuse. Despite his good looks and fine voice, just to look at him made me want to laugh; he had a droll way of story-telling. "The day war broke out," he began that afternoon - sounding just like the famous Rob Wilton, "I was on A.R.P. duty at Westminster; I had just heard Chamberlain's announcement and couldn't believe it was true - I kept telling myself that it was just a bad dream," (much rumpling of hair as he simulated a nightmare) - "or that the Premier had gone off his rocker," (imitation of mad premier with mike) - "or that it was a dreadful hoax by that unspeakable little man with the toothbrush moustache," (imitation of Hitler imitating mad premier with mike). "Then the b***** air raid siren exploded just above my head! I thought it was the Last Trump! I believed in the war after that, alright!" His name was Thorley Walters; I don't know if he ever appeared in Shakespeare, but I do know that within a few years his name appeared in lights all over the West End when he played opposite the irrepressible Cicely Courtneidge in one musical comedy after another.

He had me in stitches that afternoon and I left him reluctantly to go to the Mill, where I had a strange little mission to perform. Mrs Welsh had moved to Tiverton and had telephoned in great distress to say that she had lost some notes. Her detective story was based on Bickleigh Mill, and it was imperative to have the exact sound of the water-wheel. Was it "creak, splash, creak?" or "splash, splash, creak?" I felt an absolute lemon as I stood, notebook in hand, in front of the bemused miller. Hoteliers receive extraordinary requests!

That day was a strange one altogether, indeed for me, momentous. When I arrived back in Angela Harding's office, with my carefully recorded "splash notes", she had a letter in her hand, and seemed unaware of my noisy entrance as she perused it thoughtfully. "I've received a letter," she at last began unnecessarily, "from Cornwall. I've been offered a post at the Ferry Boat Inn on the Helford River." I was momentarily dumb-struck, then remembered that she had managed a hotel in Cornwall before coming to the Cot, to be near her grandchildren in Exeter. "That's not where you worked before, is it?" I enquired. "Oh no," she replied, "you're thinking of the Manor House at Budock Vean; this is a new place, built on the site of an old Cornish pub by a Commander Douton. It seems he's been recalled to the

Navy and, as his wife is crippled with arthritis, he's desperate to find a manageress." "Well, I wonder how he knew of you?" I exclaimed, "and how about the children?" This was more out of self-interest than altruism. I had been happy at the Fisherman's Cot and had learned much from this delightful woman. "I gather that the Pilgrims, who own Nansidwell, suggested me." She stared thoughtfully at the missive for a few more moments. "As you say, the children have to be thought of, but it is a tempting offer! I think I'll just 'phone this Commander Douton."

I left her with the telephone and went out to the kitchen. "What would I do?" I wondered. If Mrs Harding left, certainly I wouldn't remain without her.

Walters, the kitchen porter, was busy in the kitchen. He was a grey, taciturn little man and sometimes I played a private game when alone with him. I awarded myself a point each time he said anything but "Yes Miss!" He was portioning fish. "Fresh haddock - a Rokeby sauce I think, don't you Walters?" said I. "Yes Miss," he replied, inclining his head toward a dish of glistening trout. "The major again?" I asked. "Yes Miss," he replied again, adding in a sudden burst of loquacity, "they're gutted!" Ah! a point! I was triumphant, and determined to pursue my quarry before he dried up again. "What a tiny piece of beef!" I exclaimed, "that won't need much cooking!" "I'll oven at 6," he stated briefly and relapsed into silence. Two points! - not bad, but I doubted I'd get more, and after puréeing soup and decorating the desserts, I wandered out to my favourite grassy mound for a spell of serious thinking.

Though doing nothing about it, I had long been cogitating my future, waiting for some sort of sign I suppose. I'd been living in a state of limbo, which now was rudely shattered. My mind was in chaos, darting around like a new-hatched Cabbage White in search of nectar. It hovered aimlessly, then settled on our Mr Chips who was upriver, casting for trout; that redoubtable old man was at last showing his age, after losing two of his favourite Old Boys at sea.

Even in this idyllic spot the war had extruded its ugly tentacles, touching everyone with pain; particularly Mr Chips and Mabel. Mabel was still in a profound state of depression, talking as rarely as Walters. The porter emerged from the kitchen as I watched and slouched along the path towards the dining room. Hardy thought he was a trained chef brought low by alcohol; he had developed a way of life which distressed us very much, but which appeared to suit him very well. When not working or sleeping, he spent his time in a corner of the "New Inn", the ancient pub across the road - now more appropriately renamed "The Trout" - where no doubt he was just then bound for a quickie, after 'ovening' the joint.

I stared curiously, as he stopped for a moment by the French window of the dining room and looked in. Surely the old misogynist wasn't going to invite Mabel to join him? However, she failed to appear and he shrugged his shoulders and slouched off on his own.

Mrs Harding next came through the kitchen door. She seemed quite excited as she approached to tell me the results of her 'phone call. The owners of the Ferry Boat had sounded very nice she said; she had explained the predicament of Daphne and the grandchildren, but that presented no problem - there was a private flat and several empty staff rooms, so she could take them down with her. "That's wonderful," I said, "really wonderful luck for you, Hardy! I'm so glad!" Perhaps I sounded a little bleak, despite my sincere congratulations, for she laughed and squeezed my arm. "You needn't look so down in the mouth," she said, "you can come too if you like, as my deputy! There'll be far more scope for you there - there are twenty bedrooms and the Ferry Rights across the Helford and a lot of service people." Well, here was a turn up! I felt elated! My problem was solved! "Hurrah!" I exclaimed gleefully. "Look out Cornwall, here we come!" Hardy explained that the Commander had business in Exeter the next day, and she had arranged to meet him to make definite arrangements. I felt relieved and exalted, then while serving dinner, I had time for second thoughts.

Once more I was adrift in a sea of indecision, my only firm resolution to turn down Mrs Harding's tempting offer. She was flatteringly disappointed, but understanding, and I went to bed feeling virtuous but more confused than ever.

That crowded day turned into a difficult night; Walters, having failed in his mission to take Mabel to the Inn, brought some of its contents to Mabel! The pair of them got quite uproariously drunk. At 2.00 am Hardy and I had to don dressing gowns and fetch them in from the garden where they were weeping and caterwauling on each other's shoulders. We got them to bed eventually, but next morning Mabel was quite unfit for work and Walters barely ambulant.

Mrs Harding couldn't possibly leave me to cope alone while she tripped off to Exeter; reluctantly, she telephoned the Ferry Boat Inn, but the Commander proved imperturbable - he would come to the Fisherman's Cot, he said, after completing his business in Exeter, and perhaps we could provide him with lunch?

Mr Chips had been early abroad with his rod, and eggs were as yet unrationed, so I was able to produce quite a pleasant lunch of grilled trout and Queen of Puddings. Much depended I felt on this meal, and I took extra care for Hardy's sake.

The gallant Commander came, conquered and departed, leaving a sort of healthy glow in his wake! Delightful place - could see Mrs Harding ran a

48

tight ship - excellent lunch - Queen of Puddings was one of his favourites and he'd never known it better made. Very pleased to know that Mrs Harding and I were coming aboard the Ferry Boat. "But I'm not," I managed to get in at last. "I feel I should be doing something more relevant to the war effort," I explained lamely. "Ah! you feel you should be jumping into uniform, no doubt! Very commendable my dear! I must say we are very proud of our Wrens in Newcastle, but if all our lovely women-folk are caught up in war work, I can't help wondering what the devil we chaps are going to do! After all, what's the point of fighting if there's no one to come home to?" Well, I hadn't thought of that, "and a lot of our guests are servicemen," he continued, "some of them on honeymoon, poor young devils!" That remark gave me food for thought. He bent to retrieve his cap, and beamed his boyish smile direct to me as he fired the last shot in his locker - "we can soon train plotters", he said, "but a Queen of Puddings maker is something else!"

I'm as susceptible to flattery as most women, and I have another regrettable tendency; sometimes I change my mind - though I prefer to call it 'reappraising the situation'.

Anyway, Commander Douton departed whistling, leaving me somewhat fazed. Through Walters, who had set in train a strange sequence of events, it seemed my immediate future was secured, though not in a way of my own choosing. "I've been mesmerised!" I thought as I watched Mrs Harding escort our bulky visitor to his car, "but I don't <u>think</u> I regret it."

Chapter 5 - Blitzkrieg and The Dunkirk Miracle

In early May, in France, the Germans went on to the offensive. The 'Phoney War' came to an end, and to everyone's relief on May 11th a national government was formed with Churchill as Prime Minister. On the same day Mrs Harding left the Fisherman's Cot for Cornwall, and a week later I went home for a short holiday before joining her.

My departure coincided with the German blitzkrieg, which left everyone confused. The speed and brilliance of the enemy onslaught was stunning; people could speak of nothing else and the atmosphere was electric. Bruce was already in France, assigned as personal Reconnaissance Officer to the A.O.C. Northern France. Father listened almost non-stop to the wireless for fear of missing vital news, whilst Mother, I particularly remember, spent a great deal of time in her garden.

So life continued for a few days, with everyone on tenterhooks. Then brother Bruce arrived on forty-eight hours' leave. He looked exhausted, and had several plasters on his neck; his plane had been shot up, but he told Mother that he had boils due to drinking French water.

Though on the surface he was his usual cheery self, he seemed much older, as if his experiences had somehow set him apart from us stay-at-homers, and we hung on his words as he gave graphic accounts of the battle for France as seen from the air. "The German Panzer units are cutting up the allied armies like wire-cutters going through cheese!" he declared.

Indeed the German strategy was brilliant; they had made feint attacks against the impregnable Maginot Line while concentrating their main attack on the thinly defended Belgian border, where, ridiculously, it petered out. The British and Belgian defenders were quickly overwhelmed, and the Panzers roared through the Belgian Ardennes and so into Northern France.

Bruce, July 1940

The French were demoralised. Bruce amused us with tales of his French observer who couldn't believe the evidence of his own eyes and always contradicted his reports. "Ze Germans 'ave not broken through zere, our soldats fight ver' bravely, zere is no retreat!" he mimicked, adding grimly that indeed it wasn't a retreat but "a damned rout!"

It all sounded chaotic and terrifying; the main roads were blocked to the army by swarming refugees in broken-down transport all crying for "l'essence! l'essence!" as the Royal Engineers blew up the huge petrol dumps to prevent the Jerries getting the stuff. "Why don't they let the poor things have it?" we girls cried indignantly. "Because the high octane spirit would blow their engines of course!" exclaimed younger brother, John, with scorn. He worshipped Bruce, and was determined to follow him into the R.A.F., though fate, however, was to decree otherwise.

Meanwhile, Mother and Dorothy raided the precious store-cupboard while we laughed and teased and sang uproariously. The gramophone never stopped - "Little Old Lady Passing By" was Bruce's favourite, while John, I seem to recollect, favoured "The Girl in the Alice Blue Gown." (Could there be a greater contrast than that between the sentimental songs we sang in wartime and the modern raucous 'pop'?)

We went to the Odeon one night and giggled unrestrainedly as we indulged a childhood trick of flicking orange pips amongst the audience. I remember nothing of the film, only the muffled laughter which marked the underlying tension.

All too soon, Bruce was gone again, this time to get a bird's eye view of the capitulation of Belgium and the ensuing evacuation from Dunkirk. Meanwhile, we were mystified the day after his departure by an enormously long army convoy, which halted in Hill Barton Road. It stretched from Pinhoe nearly into Heavitree; all the personnel looked travel-stained and weary, so very vulnerable, so young.

In no time at all, a posse of ladies had emerged from the surrounding houses bearing trays of tea for the grateful soldiers. They were bound for Falmouth, it seemed, and thence embarkation to France. Mother was vexed to discover she had lost several tea towels in the general mêlée, but that seemed a very small complaint the following day, when to everyone's mystification, the huge convoy back-tracked through Exeter. Then on the radio we heard the news. Belgium had capitulated; no more troops were to be sent to France; the British Expeditionary Force was to be evacuated. It was a terrible blow. There were grave fears that only a small proportion of the troops could be got away. Once more, the nation was in a state of shock.

My heart was in my boots and Father strode grimly about the house, muttering about blinkered allied generals fighting a 20th century war with 19th century strategy. We had invented the tank - hadn't Father been one of the first members of that elite corps? But, surprise, surprise, we had left our enemies to exploit its terrible possibilities. The politicians, the intellectuals, the top brass, all had let the country down, and now the cream of the army was left entrapped on foreign soil. We felt sick and betrayed - all was doom and gloom.

Then a strange thing happened. Although there have been many different explanations, no one seems to know quite how it came about, but as if by some mass instinct, a huge armada of little ships set off from all the southern ports to bring our soldiers home. Even the elements were on our side; for days the Channel remained unnaturally calm, and with the help of smooth waters and the myriad small boats, the Navy was inspired to co-ordinate a miracle. How cheering it was to hear the radio bulletins! The bulk of our forces had fallen back on Dunkirk, where the series of canals and waterways surrounding the port enabled a successful rearguard action to be fought while the main body was embarked.

The small ships - the tugs and barges, the tramps and private yachts, the coasters, colliers, fire-ships and pleasure cruisers - all were invaluable. While large vessels had to queue at the only pier, the little ones were able to float almost to the beaches where they scooped up the wading men and ferried them out to the big ships.

For nine days the rescue vessels went back and forth across the Channel. Though harried by 'U' boats and the Luftwaffe, the operation was amazingly successful. Over three hundred thousand British troops were rescued and a further hundred thousand French. It was a feat of epic proportions. History books refer to it as the 'Dunkirk miracle.' The Poet Laureate called it the 'nine days' wonder', and on the eighth day I set off for the Ferry Boat.

PART II - THE HELFORD RIVER

Chapter 6 - Life at the Ferry Boat Inn

I caught a train to Plymouth where I changed and I had just set out again and the train had just reached Brunel's bridge over the Tamar when we flung ourselves on the floor as a plane roared above us, sending machine gun bullets ripping through the carriage. As we scrambled to our feet, we could see an aircraft disappearing downriver and the huge splashing from a stick of bombs which miraculously missed hitting any of the massed shipping. Everything had happened so quickly that all the passengers were temporarily stunned, then all started speaking together. "I suddenly saw it coming straight for us," said the window seat man. "Damn close shave," exclaimed someone else. "Must have been after the bridge," said a third. "Amazing that none of those ships caught it." I had to add my two-penn'orth of course. "My brother says they're rotten shots anyway." "Oh I wouldn't say that miss, not when you're at the receiving end," said Mr Window Seat quietly. I felt ashamed when I observed his plastered leg and realised for the first time that war veterans are invariably less bellicose than the stay-at-homes. "I was only whistling in the dark - I felt so frightened," I apologised. "And so say all of us!" chorused the rest of the passengers. We all became quite matey and were fascinated to learn that the wounded soldier had been rescued from Dunkirk under a hail of Luftwaffe bombs which had caused the injuries to his legs. "There was not much sign of the R.A.F.," he said. "They haven't enough planes," I said defensively and thought sadly, nay angrily of the lotus years when our forces were starved of resources for modernisation while the Jerries were arming to the teeth. "Thank God for Churchill," we all agreed, for without that great man bullying the Government and stirring the nation's conscience, we would have been even less prepared. And now he was Prime Minister, praise be!

The war was becoming uncomfortably close and I had terrible visions of mass bombing and invading Nazis cutting up our meagre forces like wire cutters going through cheese. "Do you think they will invade us?" I enquired aloud of the assorted passengers. "Well, they will have to cross the Channel first, and I dare say the Navy will have something to say about that," pronounced a sagacious fellow, and that was a comforting thought.

The Army was in disarray but certainly the Senior Service was batting well and hadn't Bruce said that at last the R.A.F. were getting new planes? Wizard new crates coming off the production lines in hundreds since Beaverbrook took over aircraft production. Doubtless the Junior Service would give a good account of itself when the time came.

The sunshine had turned to drizzle by the time I arrived at Falmouth. I was tired, hungry and distinctly low-spirited. Cornwall seemed so very grey after the cheerful brick and warm red soil of my native Devon but I perked up instantly when the cabbie asked if I would like to see the harbour. "Tisn't often," he said "that you can actually see 'istry in the making." I hadn't realised that ports so far south were involved in the evacuation, but within a few minutes the most amazing spectacle lay spread before my wondering gaze. The whole of that great natural harbour was filled with ships, so tightly packed that from where we watched it seemed impossible to put a pin between them. It was also very quiet, I recall, perhaps because of the drifting mist above the vessels, but more likely the result of exhaustion. Across the water the smothered throbs of motor launches mixed with the cries of wheeling gulls and the muted shouts of men. From somewhere out in the bay came the whooping challenge of a destroyer, forming the chorus to this modern equivalent of a Greek tragedy.

Many of the vessels flew French or Belgian flags and had arrived crammed with civilian refugees. Most of the military, I gathered, had gone to the Channel ports, and there were groups of disconsolate foreigners wandering about the streets. I shall never forget those poor people and the sad empty look in their eyes. "You should have been here a day or two since," said my informant. "Like ants they were, all over the streets, all over the beaches. The churches, cinemas and public buildings were all full up and the voluntary ladies had some job trying to feed them all until the special trains took them away."

I scarcely heard him as he prattled on. I couldn't get the sight of those poor bewildered people out of my mind as we raced along the coast to Maenporth then turned inland to the quaintly named Mawnan Smith. A mile or two further we came to Trebah Cross and then with a final rattle down a steep hill, we pulled up with a flourish before the famous Ferry Boat Inn. As I got out of the cab, a tall rather stooped man hurried away from the entrance, leaving a little apple-cheeked woman on the threshold holding in her arms a quantity of ladies' underwear. "I don't usually greet people like this," she said, ushering me into the entrance lounge. "It's Peter's fault." She indicated the black cocker spaniel lurking at her ankles. "As fast as I have been packing my boxes, he's been emptying them and scattering my things all over the beach. I couldn't think why the trunk didn't seem to be getting any fuller, and I was so embarrassed when Commander Clapp brought it all back just now." I can understand her feelings as a pair of pink Directoire knickers slithered to the floor, to the accompaniment of a gale of laughter from the group of visitors in the lounge.

Mrs Douton, for it proved to be her, was one of my surprises. I don't know what I expected but certainly not this rosy dumpling in a flowered smock and thick lisle stockings. I followed her across the crowded room buzzing with noise and activity. Tea was brought to her private sitting-room behind the reception office, and then I met Amelie, the only resident chambermaid it seemed, to care for twenty bedrooms.

Amelie took me up to my room. The whole hotel was planned like a ship. All the bedrooms opened off the southern side of the long white corridor and the numerous bathrooms and staff bedrooms faced north and overlooked the field. The bedrooms were named after sailing clippers. Mine was Pericles. "Mlle Irene Curie has been sleeping in this room!" said Amelie with pride. She was indeed a unusual chambermaid I thought, strange accent and a dark, Jewish look about her. Was she perhaps a refugee from the Jewish pogroms? "Are you exhausted? I hear there have been heaps of refugees coming here." She agreed that there had been many people, some "so difficult, particularly the actors from the Comedie Francaise - but Baron Rothschild and his party were charming and the wife of the French Ambassador to Germany is very nice indeed. She is very worried, she is here with her little boy but she has no idea where her husband is." So much tragedy - Kerry Harding was still unaccounted for and Mrs Harding looked dreadful, worn and tired like all the staff, the light quite gone from her eyes.

I could scarcely have arrived at a more dramatic moment, with a stream of misplaced people ebbing and flowing through the Ferry Boat. There were camp beds in the drawing-room and the dining-room was more like a cafeteria. Emergency rations had been distributed from somewhere. The telephone was never out of use as the distracted arrivals tried to contact friends or relatives before snatching a meal and a few hours rest. The regular holiday-makers looked on bemused "seeing 'istry" as the cabbie had remarked.

Eventually I was bidden to a late dinner with Mrs Harding, Mrs Douton and her sister Gwen. The sisters kept up a cheery flow of conversation to divert Mrs Harding from thoughts of her missing son. I was feeling rather full of myself, dying to share my experiences, particularly the moving minutes spent amongst the refugees at Falmouth. During my recital, Mrs Douton went off to take a 'phone call and came back beaming from ear to ear. "That was Courtenay!" she exclaimed - "He's very cock-a-hoop! They've taken off all our troops from Dunkirk, and a hundred thousand French, as well as countless refugees. A few days ago, they thought they would be lucky to rescue a few thousand, then all these little ships set out to help and he says the human spirit just took over." Thrilling news indeed, and wonderful to have it straight from the horse's mouth, as the Commander had been involved in co-ordinating the operation.

The two sisters set off on a stream of reminiscences. "To think that Von Ribbentrop actually sat at this table two or three years ago!" cried Mrs Douton. "Von Ribbentrop!" I couldn't have been more shaken had she lobbed a Mills bomb across the room. "He was German Ambassador to England then if you remember, and he spent a weekend with the Foxes at Glendurgan. They brought him here for dinner." "Was he awful?" I enquired. "Quite the reverse," she replied. "On the surface he was the acme of charm. The staff were all enchanted and the other guests terribly impressed - even Courtenay thought it was a feather in our cap!" "But you didn't like him?" queried Angela. "I disliked the man from the moment I set eyes on him, and when he kissed my hand it was all I could do not to snatch it away! I had the most terrible presentiment of evil. I knew from that moment we were up against some terrible force; I was convinced there was bound to be war. I told Courtenay so, but he said I was tired and overwrought." "Surely he didn't like the man!" cried Hardy and I with one voice. "Oh no! Quite the reverse. 'Slimy little runt' he called him, but he still thought I was over-reacting; he didn't want to believe of course. Two world wars within twenty years!" Her blue eyes filled with tears and I could well imagine that the generation which had endured the first Great War could scarcely have welcomed the second.

"It's very strange you should have experienced that feeling of evil," mused her sister Gwen. "I wonder if anyone else felt it?" "Strangely enough," Kathleen replied, "I was talking to that French Ambassador's wife this morning and she told me she had experienced exactly the same feeling whenever she came into contact with Hitler. And her husband said she was over-reacting!" Men were extraordinary, we all agreed, and Angela Harding thought it proved that more women should be ambassadors. "It proves to me," said Kathleen "that I should have done what I was sorely tempted to do at the time." "What was that?" "Put poison in the wretched man's soup!" she exclaimed vehemently.

I found it exhilarating to be sharing dinner with someone who, for a brief moment, had actually had the power to affect the course of history, for surely Ribbentrop was one of the cleverest of Hitler's henchmen - the architect of the plans for the military onslaught in Europe; indeed, his Moscow Treaty of Friendship with Russia, in which the two powers cynically agreed to carve up Poland between them, was the direct reason for the war because of our own treaty with that poor benighted country.

A little later, I felt a little frisson of excitement when Mrs Harding introduced me to the voluble, dark Mlle Curie who was awaiting a taxi, and then after that Mrs Douton took me in hand. She gave me a quick rundown on management procedures and introduced me to the resident staff, of whom there seemed to be regrettably few.

Out of the normal complement of fourteen, there were but five plus an excellent daily called Mrs Williams who lived in a nearby cottage. I met Maud, the cheery flaxen-haired waitress, and Ronnie the ferryman-cum-porter-cum-assistant barman. There was no cook and in place of the treasured Walters was a sulky looking lad called Fred, of whom I entertained few hopes. The bar was in the charge of the diminutive, conscientious George, and the bedrooms in the care of Amelie. There were fortunately a couple of part-time helpers to supplement the skeleton crew, but I foresaw busy times ahead, with the thirty guests, the bar, the extra meals and the ferry across the Helford to be manned.

The kitchens were wonderfully well equipped with masses of cupboards and work-tops, and the latest in pre-war electrical gadgetry including a huge washing-up machine. But it was the size of the stock-room and the amount, and the quality of the stock that really took me aback. I asked, somewhat faintly, if we had to check it, when I saw the stock-book showed a total of more than £700 (in modern money I believe that would be nigh on £20,000!!). Mrs Douton assured me that the accountant had done it when Mrs Harding arrived, and added with her characteristic quirky little smile, that the Commander always thought in terms of provisioning ships for long uncertain voyages. Rather fortunate as it happened, I thought. "Do you know," she said "that I mistakenly mentioned one January day that I hadn't made any marmalade, and he rushed off to Falmouth and returned with the greengrocer's entire stock of Sevilles!"

Actually I was beginning to feel rather cold about the feet and to wonder if I could cope with this new assignment so carelessly undertaken, but Mrs Douton looked so tired and careworn that I buttoned up my mouth. "What is Bullace jam?" I wondered aloud. "A Bullace is a wild plum," she answered. "Ah, like sloes I expect, all skin and bitters!" "That's a fair description," she giggled. "One day," - I felt a story coming on - "a beautiful yacht sailed up river, and her skipper ended up in our bar. He was an ex-Navy man with a fruit farm in Hampshire. All his produce was made into jam, and he sailed round the coast taking orders for it. After a very convivial session with my husband, he sailed away with a small order for his excellent raspberry jam and a very large order for the Bullace!" "What does it taste like?" I enquired. "Horrible!" she replied, "but I can't bring myself to throw it away!" Despite the food shortages, in nearly three years I never did find a use for that peculiar preserve!

Mrs Douton's last worry - she was leaving next morning - was for the spaniel, Peter. "The vet thought of taking him, he was going to ask his wife, but he hasn't 'phoned," she said anxiously, "and I can't possibly take him to Newcastle." "I'll look after him," I volunteered joyfully. "Oh, but he's so undisciplined," she cried, "he was an unsolicited gift you see, and we never had time to train him properly." "I don't mind, I'll look after him. I'll love him!" The little dog seemed to know that his future was being discussed. He suddenly jumped into my lap and proceeded to lick me all over.

A dog of my own! It was the final excitement in an extraordinary day; the most thrilling, emotional and action-packed day of my whole life.

Next morning I woke early to brilliant sunshine. With the fog swept away, I found the river prospect quite enchanting and couldn't scramble into my clothes quickly enough. Joined by my new canine friend, I went outside to inspect the environs of the Inn. Peter waited patiently as I appraised the long, low white building with its tile-hung upper storey; it had been cleverly contoured into the base of the steep field and had quite a continental air with its terraces ablaze with red geraniums, and adorned with Dracena palms.

The Ferry Boat Inn, Helford Passage, 1937

The water lapped gently on the foreshore, dimpling and sparkling in the early sunshine and swinging the boats, gently murmuring on their moorings. It was so beautiful, and I laughed aloud when I thought of my depression of the previous day. How could I not be happy here? My heart sang as the little dog and I, eschewing the cliff path to the east, ran gaily along the honeysuckled lane to the west. The lane is still there; it passes a little row of cottages, then continues between the hedge-bordered shingle and the pinewood gardens of some large secluded houses.

We followed the lane to Bar Beach which ends in a rocky point and a long causeway linking a taffrailed boat-house to the gardens of Bar House. A long narrow oyster boat nosed out of the creek beyond the point and chugged upriver, scarcely disturbing an elegant heron from his fishing but sending a flock of kittiwakes crying aloft. From somewhere across the river came the call of a curlew saluting the dawn. Such a beautiful and tranquil scene; it was impossible to imagine the chaos and bloody suffering just across the Channel. It was with reluctance that I retraced my steps and joined the early morning bustle of the Inn.

The next days passed in a frenetic haze. There was so much to do, so much to learn, and so little time in which to accomplish either. Mrs Douton was a sad loss. I missed her quirky humour and her common sense. Most of all, I thought, she would have known how to cope with Mrs Harding. Kerry was still missing and Operation Dynamo, as the Navy code-named the Dunkirk evacuation, had been officially wound down. Each day she looked more strained and worn. She carried out her duties with her usual efficiency but with such a distant air that one hesitated to ask her anything.

It was a relief when Daphne arrived with her three adorable children, though she too was considerably distressed. We formed a sad household though a very busy one. Most of the refugees had now departed, and although we were still full up, the English visitors were more relaxed and much easier to cope with.

Until a cook materialised, I was doomed to spend most of my time in the kitchen. Owing to the food shortages, it was a challenge to produce wholesome, attractive meals, but we were fortunate in being able to obtain fresh crabs and lobsters and a plenitude of oysters from the famous Duchy oysterage at Port Navas. We got a marvellous assortment of fresh vegetables, and fruit and eggs from the Calamansack estate further up river, which belonged to a Commander Warington-Smythe. Ronnie took a boat up twice a week and it was a sight to behold when he brought it back, laden to the gunwales with mounds of fresh produce and huge baskets of flowers.

Several days passed, days of hectic activity sadly underlaid by the tragedy of the missing Kerry, then suddenly, after all hope had been abandoned, there came a joyous 'phonecall. He was safe! Within a few hours he would arrive on leave. We were agog to hear of his adventures. His regiment had been engaged in the rearguard action to delay the Germans while the evacuation from Dunkirk went ahead. When the tattered remnants of his unit arrived at the port, it was to find the jetty reduced to rubble and all the rescue ships gone away. Exhausted and disconsolate, they bivouacked among the sand-dunes in hourly expectation of capture, when they were spotted by one of the destroyers sent out to round up any remaining stragglers. The last survivors to escape from that benighted beach, they had to spend several days aboard the destroyer until its mission was completed, which was why we had had no news.

After he returned to duty, life settled down; Hardy recovered her spirits and we began to get to know the locals - the Lewarnes, the Rickards, the Hewitts and the Williams who all lived in the pretty little Bar Road cottages, and Mrs Ursula Worth, the redoubtable chatelaine of Bar, where a long causeway led from the house to the boat-house on the beach. Hardy and I were bidden in turn for drinks. Although her house was large, Worthy and her maid were both elderly, and as most of her guests ended up at the Ferry Boat, the new management needed a thorough-going Scottish appraisal! She was forthright and shrewd but with a wonderful sense of humour. I have never forgotten the expression on her face when she described one day, shortly after the arrival of Americans in the area, the finding of an 'anti-procreation device' in her fir plantation. "If they must indulge in such practices, I wish they would not do it here!" she declared wrathfully. Rather interestingly, her house has lately been bought by Peter de Savary.

We continued to make many more friends, but I suppose my closest ones were Bert and Lucy Britton. They were comparative newcomers to the area, having arrived from Bristol in the late thirties, and had built one of the first houses on the Budock Vean estate. They were kindness itself to me; with their son in West Africa in the Colonial Service and daughter Margaret away in the W.A.A.F., I daresay they were glad of some young company - but for whatever reason, their home, Bodergy, became my second home.

Few regular visitors to the Helford escaped their hospitality. Famous musicians, sportsmen, singers, diplomats all passed through their portals, and Lucy Britton, a wise, majestic woman with a tremendous sense of humour, rarely turned a hair whomsoever Bertie brought to her door.

Another notable Helfordian was the famous Shakespearian actor, Godfrey Tearle, who frequently brought glamorous ladies to dine at the Inn. I can't claim him as a personal friend, but one day he rendered me a service - of which more later on. Certainly there was no lack of social life, just a lack of time in which to enjoy it, for the bedrooms were always filled with guests, and a constant stream of visitors passed through our door.

Chapter 7 - The Battle of Britain

After the wonderfully successful evacuation of Dunkirk, there was a brief period of rejoicing, and then a new fear gripped the country, fear of invasion. It was a very real threat because we were largely defenceless. Although most of the B.E.F. had returned home, practically all its armour had been abandoned in France. Hardy and I were reliably informed by a young attaché from the War Office that we had scarcely a score of serviceable tanks. All had been committed to France, and there they remained.

All round the coast anti-invasion defences were hurriedly erected. We escaped the first round of barbed-wire entanglements on our foreshore, but the Helford acquired its own little patrol boat whose commander came to live at the Inn. Commander Warington-Smythe was appointed our local naval officer. He had no telephone, so in the best Fred Karno spirit, we were ordered to take his messages at the Inn for onward routing by water! I believe we were allowed a small ration of petrol for this important duty - we certainly had a precious bag of sugar, firmly labelled 'For Invasion Use Only'. This was to be tipped into the petrol pump under the noses of the expected invaders I suppose, though there was precious little petrol in the pump anyway.

One night Hardy asked me to attend a meeting convened by the local Civil Defence. There were representatives from the Red Cross, the W.I., the A.R.P. and the Coastguards. The Ferry Boat was declared a collecting point in the event of an invasion alert from whence coastguards would lead us all by secret routes to safe houses further inland. We were given leaflets for making bread without yeast - but I can't remember when we were to perform this miracle - before or after the escape! All good 'Boy's Own' stuff in which I had little faith, but I suppose it made us feel that something was being done. On a more practical level, one of our wine cellars was bagged for air raid shelters. Mr Hewitt, one of the Bar Road cottagers, was appointed an air raid warden. He went on a course and took his duties very seriously. When he inspected the cellars, he pronounced them perfect - but for the lack of toilet facilities. Mrs Harding suggested that the bar cloakrooms were close at hand but, "Oh, they'd never do," he said, "you can't venture out in an air raid, ma'am, and fear do so go to the stummick!" The problem wasn't resolved, but fortunately the cellars weren't ever required.

In Cornwall life was idyllic, with hot summer days and magical moonlit nights, with few trippers to spoil the ambience. After Dunkirk, war retreated for a while, but the Cornish idyll didn't last long. In August the greatest air battle of all time began for control of the English skies. Brother Bruce was in the thick of it, attached to 59 Squadron based on Thorney Island. They flew Blenheim bomber/reconnaissance planes, nicknamed 'Flying Deathtraps' because they were difficult to escape from if shot up.

Many of our visitors came from London or the Home Counties, and they gave vivid accounts of the aerial dog-fights. They told of blazing aircraft screaming earthwards, of white parachutes descending gracefully amidst the rattle and spark of tracer bullets, of the roar and whine, the flames and spiralling smoke-trails of duelling planes, deciding Britain's fate in the azure summer skies. The losses on both sides were horrendous, but gradually the R.A.F. assumed the mastery, and despite being outnumbered two to one, destroyed more planes than they lost. Then suddenly it was all over.

By mid-September of 1940, the greatest air battle of all time was won by the R.A.F. Over nine hundred allied planes were lost, but by the Luftwaffe twice as many. Goering lost his stomach for the fight and had to change his tactics. It was a famous victory, and as usual, Churchill had the words for the occasion - "Never in the field of human conflict," he intoned, "was so much owed by so many to so few." My brother was one of them, but alas now missing.

It was many months before we knew his fate, then strangely, news came from the French resistance movement, of which we were beginning to hear quite a lot. The Germans had reported finding his empty plane shot down over Caen and they had found his dead, baled-out crew. Of the pilot there was no sign. Perhaps, the Air Ministry suggested, he was being hidden by the Resistance. Perhaps he would escape into neutral Spain. Perhaps, perhaps..... But I was not sanguine in my heart. I knew he was gone from us. The strain for my parents was terrible, though they were very good about it. It was almost a relief to hear the truth at last, for one's imagination works overtime on these occasions. Some French nuns, we heard, had reached his crashed plane before the enemy, and they had removed his body and given it honourable burial in a cemetery at Caen. They tended his grave until he was re-interred in the beautiful war cemetery at Bayeux at the end of the war. It was a heart-warming deed in a murky, dreary world, and it brought a little comfort to us all when we heard the lovely story of those brave French nuns.

Meanwhile my twenty-first birthday arrived. I was in no mood for celebration, but Hardy arranged a surprise party. She and the staff prepared party food on the quiet, and got a cake from somewhere. All our local friends came and all the visitors and staff. It so happened that we had three senior naval officers in residence, an Admiral and two 'Rears' if I remember rightly. Sailors are wonderful at parties. When the champagne came out, our three jovial Brass Hats ordered George to 'splice the mainbrace'. Rum and champers is a potent mix, and all inhibitions were quickly lost! Charades were suggested, and I shall never forget the sight of our three gallant admirals sitting in the middle of the floor, their faces as red as turkey-cocks, pretending to be sea-sick. I believe the word was 'Doldrums' but by that time nobody much cared. Auntie Lucy and Ursula Worth managed to maintain a little decorum, but nearly everyone else, including Bertie, was more than 'half-seas over' by the time they left for home.

A young army captain nabbed me on the terrace; he was waving a bottle of Kummel over his head and begged me to share it with him. "I don't like the stuff," I said, and added foolishly, "anyway we ought to be in bed!" "Jolly good idea!" he cried enthusiastically, "but firsht we musht finish this bottle! Tomorrow I go back to war!" The eternal blackmail of the soldier! I took a small sip, and he had a hefty swig, and we wandered outside and between alternate sips and swigs, we eventually found ourselves sitting on a large boulder in the middle of Bar Beach.

During a spirited rendering of "I don't know the way to go home," my companion suddenly went quiet and gently slithered off his perch. It was a night of fitful moonlight, and a sudden gleam revealed him lying in a pool of water. "Shilly man!" I called happily, "get up, you're getting wet!" There was no answer and I sobered up with a jerk as I realised the tide was coming in. Even through the haze of fifty years, I can remember the terrible panic I felt as I clambered off the rock and tried to lift his inert body, but he was a big chap and it was all I could do to keep his head out of the water. I pulled and shoved and was close to hysteria, when I heard a gentle splashing of oars and a murmur of "ahoy there!" "Oh, thank God!" I cried - or some similar exclamation - "my friend is drowning - he's drunk!" "So I observe," was the laconic reply and the owner of the voice stepped ashore and lifted the sodden bundle from the pool as if it were a baby. We had been observed by the watch keeper on the patrol boat. "I'll row you both back to the Inn - you're from the Ferry Boat, miss, aren't you?" inquired our rescuer, who I now perceived to be a giant of a man. It was a dark night, and my companion still insensible - thinking discretion was the better part of valour, I took to my heels and ran all the way back to the Inn as if the devil himself was after me!

Some of the guests were still about; the admirals helped the young officer to bed and were full of chuckles and helpful hangover tips next morning, when the poor chap tried to organise himself for his return to duty. As for me - I nearly died when I recognised our saviour in the bar the following night. I had been unpardonably rude, but he proved a genial giant and I can still recall his rumbling laugh, as he recounted the happenings of the previous night to an interested audience.

All agreed that it had been an excellent party, but in truth I never really felt quite part of it, and needless to say, was not allowed to forget my nocturnal adventures on Bar Beach for many a week!

Bar Beach, Helford Passage

Chapter 8 - Carrying On

The year 1940 ended with the terrible incendiary attack on the City of London which so badly damaged St Paul's Cathedral and destroyed eight of the beautiful Wren churches. Coventry and Bristol had been heavily bombed earlier in December; even Plymouth had minor raids.

The war was really hotting up; it was indeed fortunate that the heroic 'few' had managed to save their airfields in the Battle of Britain, or there would have been little to stop the Germans from annihilating all our major ports and cities.

Kerry came on leave and told us of an attempted invasion somewhere along the Hampshire coast. "It can't be true," Daphne said, "there's been no news of it!" "Very hush-hush!" he replied. "It was repulsed - no need to alarm the populace! We think it was a probing raid, and we gave them a hot reception, so I don't think they'll try again!" We wanted to know what had happened, but felt sick when he told us that the sea had been set afire with blazing petrol which left a trail of burnt bodies all along the shore. How horrible it all was, for friend and foe alike. For how much longer, we wondered, would the carnage have to be endured? For many more years did we but know. It was a question of hanging on until America declared for the allies; who could blame her for holding back? At least they were helpful with war supplies and anyone with American connections received regular parcels of food and other necessities.

Meanwhile our government was preparing for a long slog. Gradually the whole country was turned into a vast war production machine, frivolities were out, the few beautiful products were sent to America to earn much needed cash; strangely, for many people, one of the hardest things to bear as the war progressed was the lack of coloured china! Most of us need a modicum of beauty in our lives and frugal food seemed even less appetising when served on thick white plates!

Everything was recycled, tins, paper, scrap iron, bottles; clothing was patched and darned, hems taken up or down to suit the various wearers; all household scraps were composted or fed to hens or pigs in return for a precious egg or two or a piece of pork. War time England - and the rest of Europe, no doubt - was a paradise for the Greens!

It also saw an awakening of the national conscience; people were shocked at the malnourishment of many of the little evacuees, and also at finding that some had never slept in proper beds, nor understood simple hygiene or had proper clothing. If the war had a silver lining, surely it was the determination to eradicate this dire poverty when it ended.

But first the war had to be won. All talents were enlisted. As well as mathematicians, champion crossword puzzlers and chess players, for example, were found to make brilliant code-breakers and were drafted to work at Bletchley with the Enigma and Ultra machines. Somewhere in England a special unit of skilful packers worked for years on survival packs used by servicemen on secret missions; by D-Day these packs had been reduced to an irreducible minimum, and were issued to all troops on the invasion craft - they included sick bags, soap and toilet paper as well as hard rations. Carrier pigeons were occasionally used for top secret messages, and specially trained dogs for detecting survivors amongst bomb ruins. Artists devised camouflage schemes, entertainers joined E.N.S.A. I well remember a most interesting man who came to the Ferry Boat for a holiday; he was blind and had developed a remarkable sixth sense - he was a human lie detector! He worked for one of the intelligence services, and was invaluable when captured Germans were being interrogated.

There were diverse problems to be solved - the storage of vast quantities of ammunition for instance. I doubt if many East Devonians knew that their beloved Woodbury Common was one huge ammunition dump; the heathland was honeycombed with tunnels to store the arms, carefully guarded by camouflaged soldiers of the Royal Army Ordnance Corps. I expect such dumps existed all over England in unexpected places.

It is amazing that so many secrets were so well kept - "Careless talk costs lives!" proclaimed the propaganda posters and most citizens took the message seriously.

All over the country small engineering workshops were turned over to making components for war. An Uncle with large automobile workshops in Tunbridge Wells produced complicated gear-boxes for tanks, and he told Mother, after the war was over, that the place was run by the Unions. The shop steward was an absolute menace until Germany turned against Russia. Then the workers became more co-operative, but constantly reminded my Uncle that he would no longer be the boss when the Russkies beat the Germans!

These perverted fellows seemed to give no thought to their own compatriots who were suffering and dying and drowning to stop the Jerries starving us to death, and blasting our cities to kingdom come!

Chapter 9 - The Unspeakable Haw-Haw

One of the arch traitors of World War II was William Joyce, the Englishman turned German propagandist, nicknamed 'Lord Haw-Haw' because of his affected voice. He caused much anguish in our small corner when the Commander of the Falmouth guard ship, Commander Ireland, took rooms at the Ferry Boat for himself, his wife and small son. He was a quiet, kindly man and we grew to like him and his pleasant wife and little son, Christopher. After some months with us, they were 'part of the family'.

Then disaster struck. Early one morning, several of us were awakened by an explosion somewhere out in the bay. "Oh dear, another ship gone," I thought with dismay, then turned over and sank back into sleep.

In the morning, Mrs Ireland was summoned to Falmouth to hear tragic news. The guard ship had struck a mine and gone down with all hands. Mrs Ireland was shattered, of course, particularly next day when the unspeakable Haw-Haw announced on the German radio that her husband wasn't dead, but taken prisoner by a German 'U' boat which had torpedoed his ship. The Admiralty said it was impossible, no 'U' boat had surfaced in the area, definitely the ship had been mined. The poor widow didn't know what to believe. Haw-Haw was a sadistic swine; normally we listened to his broadcasts with amusement and derision, but he really put the boot in this time, and it compounded the tragedy for the bereaved family.

Spy mania became rampant. How could the wretched traitor have known the name of the C.O. on the wrecked vessel? The air was heavy with suspicion, and anyone with foreign connections was suspect - our Amelie, Dr Strecher, an old gardener who had a German Mother - all were whispered against.

An old retired Admiral, who had served in naval intelligence in the First World War, was making a prolonged visit at the time. I fear he fuelled the flames - he was always spotting mysterious lights (usually traced to careless householders) - and he found the behaviour of some of our Cornish odd-balls suspicious in the extreme. One day I actually found him examining foot-prints on the cliff path with a spy glass! Eventually the furore died down, the sad widow abandoned hope when no further word came of her husband, and she took her departure with her little son.

Other concerns came to the fore, some happy, some sad, in the bittersweet manner of wartime. Dear Maud started 'walking out' with a handsome young man from Helford, one Deacon Rickards, nephew to Ernie Rickards of Bar Road. Deacon later joined the Helford flotilla, of which more will be written later in this book. Maud was walking on air but Daphne and I were becoming increasingly anxious about Mrs Harding. She declared she was perfectly well but we knew she was suffering terribly from insomnia and excruciating bouts of indigestion.

She still kept her sense of humour, however, and was vastly amused by an inoffensive middle-aged couple who arrived on honeymoon. The Ferry Boat was a famous place for honeymoons, but this bridegroom was so afraid Hardy would assume the worst when his bride produced a ration book still in her maiden name that he fetched the marriage-lines for her perusal! The fact that they were such a conventional pair added to the piquancy of the situation, particularly as another couple staying at the time, the C.B.'s (of whom more later), had booked two rooms in different names and then asked if we could provide communicating doors!

Deacon Rickards, Maud's fiancé

Such minor events caused much amusement, but in the March of that year, 1941, the whole nation had cause for great rejoicing. Churchill and Roosevelt signed the generous American Lease/Lend agreement which meant the Yanks would send us much needed food and war equipment in return for British assets in America. The agreement saved us from near starvation and the sight of tinned fruit, dried egg and the ubiquitous 'spam' on the grocer's shelves filled housewives with ecstasy! Endless queues would form until the shelves were emptied when there would be much ill-feeling among the 'have-nots'. Eventually the Ministry of Food under the brilliant Lord Woolton introduced a points system which was much fairer, particularly for country-folk like us who were unable to prowl round the shops each day.

Chapter 10 - Foreshadows of Death

By mid-April, Angela Harding was clearly ill, and Daphne and I persuaded her to see her doctor. He sent her to see a specialist who recommended an immediate operation. I wrote an anxious note to the Doutons and received a telegram which read "Complete trust in you and staff. Stop. Carry on until I get leave. Douton". This massaged my ego, but was not otherwise very helpful. However, sister Freda had fortunately just completed a secretarial course and had a few weeks before starting on a banking career. Thankfully, she agreed to come and help us.

Within a few days of seeing her surgeon, Hardy was summoned to the hospital, and gave me a crash course in 'what every good hotelier ought to know'. Though I was familiar with house rules and most aspects of the business, the mysteries of the Log book, the Spirits book and the Black book were swiftly unravelled and as quickly forgotten. Here was the safe key, there were the keys to the desk drawers, those were the ones for the cellars. In between cooking the meals, I must remember to be around to greet the new guests, inspect the bedrooms, do the flowers, keep an eye on the kitchen, appear punctually in the bar to cash up at night, have the bills ready for departing guests and the bedroom lists for the chambermaids; not forgetting the boiler fuel, the baker, the butcher, the candlestick maker, the beer - phew!! Fortunately the taxi arrived before my pate was completely addled, and I waved her off to hospital with Daphne.

Back in the office I looked again at the confidential books. The Spirits book was Greek to me, the Log book fascinating but ancient history, as there were no entries since the Commander's departure - but the Black book held my attention. It had to be consulted before any bookings were accepted and it was easy to see why it was kept under lock and key - it was downright libellous! The initials N.B.G. constantly recurred - what could they mean I enquired in my next letter to Newcastle? Back came the reply by telegram, "Silly girl, no bloody good of course. Stop. Douton".

I was furious! How could he? He knew the postmistress listened to all the 'phone calls and read the telegrams. The contents of this one would by now be common knowledge. And Postie was just as bad. He had a long round, from Mawnan to Budock Vean, to the Passage, across the cliffs to Durgan and heaven knows where else. He passed the time inspecting unsealed envelopes and reading all the postcards. "Fancy George writin' that!" he exclaimed indignantly one morning as he handed me the post.

George was on holiday and his simple message read "Having a lovely time. Shan't want to come back to work." "He works jolly hard," I said, "but under the circumstances I shall be relieved when he arrives back tomorrow." "Managin' alright?" enquired the postman. "Yes, but I could do with more confidentiality from the Post Office!" I said with feeling. Whistling in the wind of course, as I complained to Daphne. More news was disseminated by the postal staff than by the postal system it seemed. I'd no doubt that the Commander's telegrams, George's postcard and the number of buff envelopes - "I 'ope she's keeping up with them there bills" - would all have been chewed over at ensuing ports of call.

Freda arrived just in time. I was at my wit's end, helping to cook the meals by day and 'cooking the books' at night! Almost immediately she arrived, she was greeted by a bomb! "Don't worry, it's one of ours," she assured an ashen-faced Maud as an aeroplane flew down-river. She was promptly contradicted by the huge splash of an exploding bomb which mercifully fell into the water and not on land.

Freda soon got the bookwork under control. It was great to have her help and companionship, and as Angela was making progress after her operation, I felt we had a fair wind at last.

But life was not without incident, and one afternoon when I was manning the ferry for Ronnie, I had a shattering experience. I had Daphne's three little ones in the boat; one minute we were chuckling and laughing together, then came a dark shadow and a plane roared out of the sun and spattered the water around us with machine gun bullets. We were just arriving at the Point and at first I was so startled and then so angry that I could scarcely get a line to the waiting passengers. Aghast, they had watched the incident, then one of them, a frequent customer, Godfrey Tearle, seized the line and pulled us ashore. He was absolutely furious and insisted on rowing the ferry back himself.

He was ill repaid for his kindness. A few days later he brought a party to dine and ordered champagne. Fred was despatched to fetch it from the bar, and brought it back already opened by a trying-to-be-helpful, but thoughtless, Ronnie. I heard an explosive oath through the hatch to the dining-room and, to my horror, saw the precious bubbly cascading into the ice-pail. It was my painful duty to have to apologise and I entered the dining-room with a sinking heart. "I'm dreadfully sorry, Mr Tearle," I began, "as you know we have no wine waiter. I'll send for another bottle." The great actor was nothing if not gallant, and was already nicely oiled. "Oh, think nothing of it, dear girl," he declaimed, and continued in his best Shakespearian tones, "after all, there *is* a war on. Outside the tempest rages but within the good wine floweth and may yet be drinkable!" The other guests were vastly entertained. 'All the world's a stage,' I thought that evening, and we were privileged with seats in the front row of the stalls.

On the night of the extraordinary arrival of Rudolf Hess in Scotland, London suffered another terrible incendiary attack, which set in motion another great exodus. To our joy, a little family came to Helford Passage. It's an ill wind - because of the horrific aerial attacks, we acquired Winnie, a former shop assistant who turned into a first-class chambermaid, and her carrot-haired niece who had an unfashionable desire to be a cook. She was but sixteen years old and she was a wonder, a born cook who soon absorbed all I could teach her. She tamed the recalcitrant Fred and within weeks was the undisputed queen of the kitchen.

The arrival of Winnie and Réné was a miracle. It seemed that Angela's recuperation would be less rapid than we had hoped, and Freda's time with us was limited. I don't know how I would have coped. Meanwhile, they had graphic and astonishing tales of the London blitzes, of the extraordinary nights spent in the shelters, of the terrible destruction and loss of life, and when incendiary bombs were falling, it became the practice for householders to stay waiting in their doorways with buckets of ashes, ready to rush out to douse the devices and then rush back again. What guts those people had - how sheltered we were in our rural retreat.

Summer arrived. The Inn was crammed to the gunwales, early morning arrivals often being accommodated in the private flat for a few hours until their rooms were free. The dining-room was fully booked, the bar till rang merrily. Sometimes on Friday visits to Falmouth, I had as much as £1,000 to bank. I used to put the money at the bottom of my shopping basket covered over with a newspaper. Despite the war, there was very little risk of being robbed, and mugging was unknown.

These weekly shopping trips were a welcome break from the daily round. Usually I took Mr Bampfylde's bus. It was an ancient rattly vehicle but had the useful property of seeming elasticity - there was always room for just one more. Mr Bampfylde drove with great panache! The trip was quite exciting as we lurched round corners and tore down hills at breakneck speed, and made sudden dramatic stops. The passengers breathed a collective sigh of relief as he drew up with a flourish on the Moor at Falmouth and we were able to tumble out. He was wall-eyed, which probably explained the near-misses, and bandy-legged which might have had something to do with the crashing gears. He was a character, a life-line for country folk unable to make frequent trips to Falmouth to collect things like library books, laundry and groceries.

One particular day, everything were awry after the banking. I couldn't find any interesting titbits in the food shops, and had no spare coupons for clothes. I decided to join Auntie Lucy and Bert at the "Brains Trust" at the Olde Englishe Tea Roomes. The B.T. was a collection of friends who met for coffee and gossip on a Friday morning; that day Howard Spring joined the group and there was indignant talk about the bolshie dock workers; these dockers posted their own look-outs who signalled them to take shelter every time a plane was spotted, be it friend or foe. This wasted hours of time and caused fury among the seamen. Somehow the conversation turned to politics and government; Howard said that any form of government was a kind of tyranny, but that a tyranny of the right was preferable to the left. I was surprised at this remark from the author of "Fame is the Spur" and I said so. He was about to expound his philosophy when I suffered another annoyance. A mutual friend rushed in waving a bag of oranges - "one for each book so long as stocks last!" she cried. Semantics came second to comestibles, and there was a lemming-like rush to the greengrocers. "I think of nothing but food," I thought crossly as I entered the grocers, "or lack of it," I amended as I came out empty-handed. Mrs Gray had spread the news too well.

The day ended with a disastrous visit to the hospital, where Angela Harding looked so ill that I had a good cry in the hospital loo before I felt able to face the world again. That was the day I began to wonder if she would get well again, and I was in no mood to enter into the conversation on the homeward bus, either to congratulate the triumphant shoppers brandishing their spoils, or to commiserate with the 'fruitless' ones.

But at Mawnan Smith there was a little diversion which raised my spirits considerably. Who - or what - should be sitting at the bus stop but Peter! As the last passenger alighted he hopped on the bus, and pretending not to see me, flopped down beside Mr Bampfylde. "Well!" I expostulated. "Oh, he often waits for me here," said the old man complacently. "E'll get off at Trebah Cross." And he did. The little dog raced down the hill and sat on the terrace ready to welcome me as if he hadn't seen me all day! He was very male, I decided. He had his private life which he kept to himself, and his public one which he allowed me to share. He knew all the best cooks and all the prettiest bitches for miles around; he often crossed the river in the ferry in pursuit of same, and now I had discovered, when tired after a day of junketing around, he cadged lifts home with Mr Bampfylde! He certainly had a wonderful life! He came home punctually for his evening meal, then padded into the bar to greet the regulars and to lap up the beer slops in the basins under the taps. After exhausting the amenities of the bar, he would retire to the office and sleep until it was time for our evening stroll.

He was indeed a character, that little spaniel. Intelligent, but as Mrs Douton had said, quite undisciplined - an absolute rascal in fact, but I loved him dearly. I groomed him until his coat gleamed like satin, and fed him on brown bread and vegetables and meat scraps. Titbits were severely discouraged. As a result, he was active and joyous, but led a wasted life for with training he would have made an excellent gun dog.

Something is sadly amiss with the modern Cocker; his head has become narrow and pointed, with little room for brains, and his ears so long and heavy that he can scarcely lift his head. Perhaps this accounts for the uncertain temper? Gone, and much regretted, are the merry little dogs I used to know and love.

Shortly after Peter's escapade, we had a visit from a rather shifty gentleman. He wanted to know if a Mr C.B. had stayed with us. I replied that he had. "Alone?" asked the shifty gent. "With a friend," I replied, then dashed his hopes by mentioning the single rooms. He wanted to speak to the chambermaid, but I told him, untruthfully I regret to say, that she was off-duty. Knowing the Commander's dislike of 'hanky-panky' and undesirable publicity, I sent the fellow packing as quickly as possible. Then, "he's sure to try the bar," I thought and flew round the back way and caught George's eye just as the 'S.G.' was entering the door. After putting the reliable George in the picture, I then went to warn the rest of the staff.

The persistent fellow stayed for lunch but he got nothing out of Maud or any of our loyal staff. It was a narrow squeak. Some months later the C.B. divorce hit the headlines but fortunately there was no mention of the Ferry Boat.

Freda had returned home when Mrs Harding's doctor dropped his bombshell. She was terminally ill. Daphne had to break the news to Kerry and I wrote at once to the Doutons. The inevitable telegram arrived - "Very sorry to receive news. Stop. Confident you and staff will cope until leave. Stop. Douton".

We did our best but problems mounted. The electrician failed to come despite many promises, and one by one our various gadgets packed up - sometimes with dangerous consequences, like the day Winnie's floor polisher became live. It refused to relinquish her hand and followed her round the room as she tried frantically to free herself. She collapsed with shock when Maud and I arrived and switched off the power. She had to go to bed for several days, thus compounding the staff shortage.

Then the food situation worsened. We could no longer obtain poultry and eggs from Calamansack; under new regulations they had to go direct to the Food Ministry. That was a great blow, and I was wearily sitting in the office one evening, trying to plan menus, when George came in to say that "a gent in the bar would like a word".

The "gent" proved to be a dealer. He offered me a side of lamb, and though I blinked at the price, I accepted it with joy, and had a good gloat as I stacked it in the fridge. The pleasure soon turned sour. A few days later the dealer offered me rump steak at an astronomical price and was very annoyed when I demurred. "Got it special for you," he said. "But I didn't ask for it," I replied. "If you take one lot it means you're committed," he said. "I'll be in at the weekend and I'll expect 'ee to take it then." It was a profound shock to realise I was dealing with a blackmailer. I couldn't think what to do.

Then the telephone rang. It was Kathleen, to say that the Commander had leave, and that they would be coming down in a few days. Like a giant refreshed, next day when my blackmailer asked if I would take his meat, I gaily answered, "No!". After these many years I can visualise his brutish face and the purple flush which gradually suffused it. "You'll hear more about this," he exclaimed in fury. "I ain't finished with you yet!" "Well," I replied, "you can take it up with the Commander - he's coming on leave next week." The man gulped his ale, and turned on his heel, and we didn't see him again for many a month. The 'Comm' was well known for his straight dealing and he had a particular dislike of war profiteers.

The Doutons were also very popular with their employees who were all lined up in best bib and tucker to greet them the next week. I felt happier than for weeks past; the thought of being able to shed my responsibilities for the next two weeks was wonderful, and I too grinned from ear to ear as the taxi arrived at the door.

"Why Courtenay, we needn't have worried!" cried Mrs Douton. "Everyone looks so happy and it's looking lovely everywhere!" "Well done! Well done indeed!" cried her hearty spouse. "George, Maud, Amelie, Ronnie!" They shook hands all round and were first introduced to Winnie and Réné, and then to a few of the guests who were lingering in the lounge.

A ship's inspection followed with me as First Lieutenant, slightly aft of the Commander to start with, then rapidly coming abreast as I got carried away with my list of complaints. "The bar is awfully shabby." "Hasn't Wilf Pascoe been?" "No, and the electrician won't come either." "I'll soon see about that!" "And the food is getting so difficult." "Did the guests complain?" "Well, not often. We have lobsters of course, but the wet fish is awful!" "Perhaps I'd heard about the war at sea?" If only the ground would have opened and swallowed me up! How could I have been so insensitive? For the Commander was a Commodore of east coast convoys, providing naval protection for the food ships and merchantmen running the gauntlet of the U-boat blockade from Newcastle to "Bomb Alley" in the Channel where the Luftwaffe took over. Night after night he spent at sea, rarely able to leave the bridge for sleep or proper meals; and wondering how much longer his luck would hold before his ship joined the list of blazing victims.

And here was I complaining that we couldn't get fresh fish but had to make do with lobster! Words failed me, I've rarely felt so ashamed, but the Commander roared with laughter. "You needn't look so woebegone!" he exclaimed. "We don't expect plaudits for doing our duty. I'm sorry I'm not Lord Woolton, but I've got one or two other ideas which may help."

By now we'd arrived at the private sitting-room and Maud was setting down a tray of tea. "Well, well, like old times, eh Maud? Do you know Miss Reynolds, Maud came to us straight from school when we first opened in '37." Maud blushed and withdrew, and my employers and I sat down for tea and a long discussion. The books weren't a problem - the accountant could send someone out once or twice a month; that was a relief, those books haunted me. "And couldn't Daphne Harding to a regular stint in Reception?" "Well, the boys are rather a handful," I said. Mrs Douton said she thought she knew of a little school. The electrician was telephoned next. "Well sir, yes sir, of course sir, first thing in the morning sir!" I could have murdered the man after his weeks of prevarication, but gradually the dark clouds rolled away or became little fluffy white ones.

"It's all ticking over splendidly and I'm delighted with the reservations," announced my employer. "But how do you manage all the correspondence?" Well, I'd evolved a little scheme - the letters were answered by post of course, but fortunately many of the enquiries now came by 'phone or telegram. I waited till the small hours when the crowded lines were usually free and sent off all the replies in one batch. "The night operator is very helpful," I confided. "He's a master of compression, saves us pounds - and sometimes if I'm late, he rings me in case I've forgotten." The Doutons both roared with laughter. I'd grown so used to the arrangement, I'd overlooked its humorous aspect. "It works very well," said I defensively. "Oh I'm sure it does!" beamed the Commander. "Is this paragon on the payroll?" I had to join in the merriment but ceased further revelations. Sometimes, you see, if there were many enquiries for the same date, I discussed the most likely ones with my telephone friend. The winners were those who wrote the most interesting letters or despatched the wittiest telegrams, which was perhaps not the most scientific method of filling the Inn!

Anyway, I held my tongue and the Commander put the booking chart away. "That's enough for today I think", he said. "It's a great relief to see our trust has not been misplaced, eh Kathleen? Really a tremendous relief! And now, as it seems that our poor Mrs Harding is not going to recover, I think it's time we made your position here official. We'd like to make you our Manageress. What about it, eh?"

Was it only eighteen months ago that I had been thought incapable of taking the job of Under-Matron to a lot of giggling school girls? 'Life is a roundabout,' I thought and I wept inwardly for my dying instructress. At the same time, I felt very relieved and happy and as I left them, I burst into song for the first time in months.

75

There was yet another bridge to cross, however, one to which I had not given a thought until the Commander asked if he could join Peter and I one evening as we set off on our usual 'unwinding' walk. We walked to Durgan and towards the spectacular panorama of sea and cliff which lies beyond, where we stopped to admire the sunset. It was a tranquil one of rosy pinks and mauves shot through with gold, mirrored in the gently rippling water.

"Isn't it breathtaking?" I sighed. "I have always wanted to travel, but could there be anywhere in the world more beautiful than this?" The Commander said he doubted it, adding that he'd done his share of rubber-necking! His experiences went back to the days of sail; in peacetime and in war he'd travelled the oceans of the world by means of wind or steam. "We chaps dream of scenes like this," he said wistfully as he puffed away at his pipe. "There's no place like the old country and no women in the world to compare with our English roses. However, there's something else we have to discuss." He still seemed reluctant to come to the point, and I can remember him shaking out his pipe before suddenly exclaiming, "You've got to hold the licence you know!" I was flabbergasted. "I'm afraid there's no way out. I've consulted the legal eagles. By law the licensee must live on the premises, and that means you, my dear."

I was silent. Why, until visiting the New Inn at Bickleigh Bridge, I'd never even been inside a pub - it simply wasn't done before the war. And now - to be the licensee. "You're very young of course," he continued. "I've had a word with Cuthbert Fox, you know, our local J.P." "Yes, Ribbentrop's host, they often come for meals." "So he said, and fortunately he's quite impressed. Said he thought the place would go to pot when Mrs Harding became ill. Anyway, he's willing to give you a good reference and recommends you to get as many more as possible, particularly from people who have known you for years." "Well, I don't imagine my parents will be enchanted," I said, "but of course I am of age." "We live in changing times Nora," he sighed. "I hope they won't be upset. The Ferry Boat will be up the creek without a paddle if you don't get that licence."

I rang home that very night, and to my surprise, my parents weren't at all upset. They were more 'with it' than I. "We live in changing times," pronounced Father, echoing the Commander, and Mother was immediately practical. She thought the vicar would write a suitable letter, likewise my old headmistress and an alderman friend. Soon I had a clutch of enthusiastic testimonials which were despatched with the appropriate forms, then there was an interlude before the next licensing sessions.

The Doutons returned to Newcastle, and a few weeks later I was bidden to court. Bertie Britton offered to take me, to the displeasure of the local bobby who was young and helpful, but slightly lacking in humour. "Not a good choice if I may say so, miss," he pronounced gravely. "He's up for a blackout offence you know." It was typical of Bertie not to have told me that. "But there's no one else," I said, adding facetiously, "I won't sit too close to him." "That will be best," said my friendly P.C. solemnly.

Uncle Bert and I entered the court room on the appropriate day, and had just settled ourselves comfortably when we were all sent out again. The first case concerned a young man accused of 'making a public nuisance of himself'. "What does it mean?" I asked Bertie, but he blushed deeply and said he didn't know. Then we returned to court. Bertie was lectured and fined, then my application came up. The magistrates questioned me closely and studied the documents, then the chairman cleared his throat and said he hoped I understood the responsibility of holding a liquor licence, and of course I was very young - but the Commander was away serving his country, etc etc. 'Granted for a trial period of three months'.

As Ronnie and I chugged up to Port Navas a day or two later, we were hailed across the water by the South African High Commissioner. "How's the youngest licensee today?" he yelled. I could have murdered him. "Not so loud, Mr Waterson. It makes me feel self-conscious," I called back. He only laughed and invited me to dinner. "The Brittons are coming, and Juta's down, so you will have a dancing partner." This was a reference to my first terpsichorean encounter with the gallant Colonel Juta. The delightful fellow was more accustomed to partnering diplomatic dowagers than young ladies. On that occasion he had started off at the pace of a dignified snail, then suddenly remembering my comparative youth, had whirled me round the floor like a demented dervish till we both landed in a heap on the floor.

The party as usual was lovely, the conversation witty and illuminating. Then H.E. explained much of the early history of South Africa and the role of Field Marshal Smuts in bringing about the rapprochement between the Boers and the English. "There is a greater task ahead," he said, for once speaking gravely. "There is so much to do for the blacks; we are planning a special university and much better education, for the potential of our country is enormous. With proper planning, there can be work and opportunity for everyone, black, white or coloured." He got quite carried away and I was spellbound. He was planning to build a great hotel in his vineyard and asked me to go out there after the war to help run it. Had I not married I might well have done so, but I'm glad I didn't, because after all, the wonderful intentions came to nothing, the Nationalists came to power in 1948 and introduced the obnoxious creed of apartheid. But that night those delightful South Africans dreamed wonderful dreams and we were all swept up in their optimism.

Now, nearly sixty years later, we seem to have come full circle, with the first free elections for black and white in South Africa. Let us hope that a new, more just era is opening out there.

Chapter 11 - The Helford Flotilla

About this time, a strange flotilla, including a French tunnyman, appeared in the river. Ridifarne, one of the Bar Road houses, was lent out to the Navy by the Bickford Smiths and a Commander Holdsworth moved in with his wife Mary and assorted naval personnel. Ostensibly they formed a cartography unit, but we all wondered what the French vessel had to do with such work, and where the old Frenchman, one Pierre Guillet, fitted in.

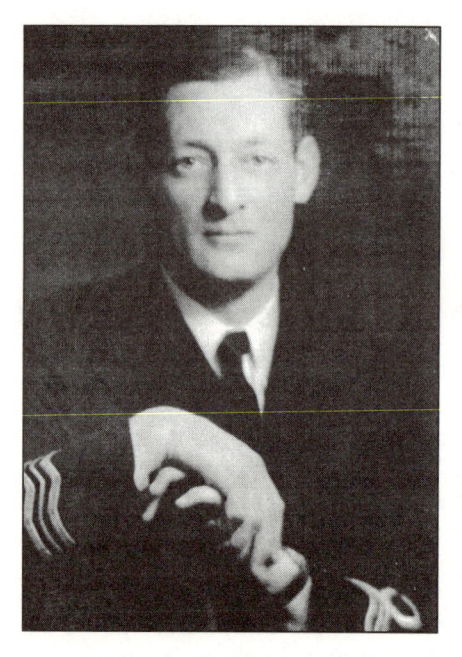

Gerard Holdsworth
Commander, Helford Flotilla

Pierre Guillet
Helford Flotilla

The Holdsworths proved charming. They often came for meals and the crews of the assorted vessels under Gerard Holdsworth's command spent much of their time in our bar. Pierre spoke no English and he wept one night when I addressed him in French. He was lonely, said his constant companion, Sgt Peake, who seemed upset at the old man's plight, but most of the other members of this unusual outfit were a cheery lot, particularly the Guernsey skipper, Bunny Newton. He was a regular buccaneer in appearance, with a dark beard and wicked twinkling eyes. His wife was housekeeper at Ridifarne, the two having somehow escaped from Guernsey when it was occupied by the Germans. Bunny had been born with his feet in the water, his family having been pilots and ferry owners for generations.

The new unit created quite a stir when it arrived but the personnel soon became part of the everyday scene. Sometimes conferences were held at Ridifarne, and the official visitors used to have rooms at the Ferry Boat. There was a particular naval officer I was to hear more of later called Captain Slocum.

I was surprised one day when two of the sailors from 'Mutin' appeared at the back door with a great panful of pilchards. "Manna from heaven!" I exclaimed, "but how did you come by them?" They looked rather sheepish as they explained that, being somewhat bored, they had tossed a hand grenade overboard, "and all these fish came floating to the surface." I felt it prudent to resist further questioning; the sailors departed with pocket money and I put "Detonated Pilchards" on the breakfast menu. This amused the guests, but I had a little doubt at the back of my mind. Why did cartographers need detonators?

There was something mysterious about that patrol, I felt. I felt it in my bones. That night I couldn't sleep; as I counted the millionth sheep, I thought I heard the muffled throb of a marine engine. I slipped out of bed, and could just make out the shape of a vessel proceeding down-river. I was pretty sure it was 'Mutin'. 'Mutin' - sneaking out at night with muffled engines - what cloak and dagger stuff was this?

The reason dawned in a blinding flash - they were going to France of course. Our cartographers were running a secret boat service across the Channel. I was sure I had hit on the secret of Ridifarne, of the French crabbers, of old Pierre; everything fitted into place and I was bursting to confide in someone. But there was no one to confide in. Hardy was the only one and she was desperately ill. It was useless trying to sleep again, and as the dawn crept across the sky, I dressed and set off across the cliffs with Peter. The little dog was enchanted to be abroad so early and ran happily through the dew-spangled grass as the sun rose in a sort of pearl haze.

The river had been comparatively quiet the previous evening, but the wind was now rapidly strengthening, and I wondered how 'Mutin' was faring, and who was aboard her, and whither her destination. Probably she had secret agents aboard. Oh dear, what dangerous lives these people led. I felt very disturbed about it.

The little dog and I walked on and on, and were well past Durgan when the rapidly rising wind forced us to return. The pair of us were

'Mutin'
Helford Flotilla

wafted back along the path like driven leaves. A strong wind is a force to be reckoned with on the Helford as it drives straight up the funnel of the estuary.

A coastguard stood on the path ahead, scarcely able to stand as he trained his glasses on some object at the base of the cliff. "What's up?" I called. "There's a mine down there!" he yelled back. "A mine!" I cried in alarm - it was but fifty yards from the Inn. "Yes, must have drifted in with the easterly. I'm waiting for the Army. The area will have to be sealed off until the bomb squad can deal with it. Meanwhile, you'd better warn everyone in the Passage to keep their windows open."

I sped down to spread the news. A strong east wind was hazard enough, and I was glad to see that Ronnie and Fred had already hauled up the boats - but an exploding mine would certainly demolish us, open windows or no!

We felt a little safer when a platoon of young soldiers arrived, and encamped themselves on the cliff top. They took turns to watch over the restless mine bobbing about in the little pool at its foot, and we felt very sorry for them. It was such a dangerous, monotonous task, but with the extraordinary adaptability of the human race, we soon got used to the situation.

It made a good topic of conversation next time I visited Mary Holdsworth. I couldn't tell her that I suspected the secret life going on in her home. I liked her very much; she was intelligent, petite and darkly pretty; we had reached a certain level of friendship, swapping recipes and local gossip.

The atmosphere in her home was so calm and domesticated, with Mrs Newton going quietly about her duties, occasional seamen popping in to see their C.O., Mary and I playing with the cats. How could it possibly be the nest of intrigue I suspected? And how could its chatelaine, who must have suffered agonies when Gerry went out on his missions, preserve such a picture of innocent domesticity? She was indeed a most courageous and resourceful woman.

Some time later, the Mother of Gerard's first wife announced her imminent arrival with his little daughter. Gerard was clearly anxious when he came to enquire about accommodation, and just as plainly delighted when I told him I could only manage to have them for three days. Undeterred at this news, the Mother-in-law, the Countess of Cathcart, presumably unaware of the cat's cradle into which she had loosed the little girl, badgered our Mrs Williams into renting her spare bedroom. "T'will serve us very well," she said, and arranged to stay for two weeks.

She was a charming though determined woman, and not at all happy with her visit. "It's too bad of Gerard," she confided to my Mother, who was staying at the time with Father. "He's hardly seen the child since the war began, and now I've brought her all the way from Scotland and we've scarcely seen him at all! I can't make out what's going on." Mother thought it quite extraordinary, and I daren't enlighten them.

Eventually the Grandmother and the little daughter departed, the Countess still breathing fire, and the little girl no doubt unhappy at leaving her Father. There must have been sighs of relief at Ridifarne, but to me it seemed very sad. Domestic happiness is the first casualty of war.

The Ferry Boat attracted visitors from all walks of life - from millionaires to bank clerks, from mandarins of the Civil Service to the very lowest grades, from all branches of the armed forces, and household names from stage, screen and radio.

The most energetic of our visitors was certainly Michael Powell, the English film director then on the threshold of his great career, who produced a stream of delightful films in collaboration with Emeric Pressburger.

At the time of his visit, Michael had just finished "The 49th Parallel". Though supposedly on holiday, he never relaxed for one minute, and treated the Inn as if it were his film studio. The man was on wires; he completely monopolised my office as he fixed up the distribution rights of his films all over the world. We quarrelled vigorously one morning over his invasion, and eventually came to a one-sided agreement - I still found it hard to get at the telephone, but at least he planted his bottom on one side only of the office desk, while I made up accounts on the other. "Your film had better be good," I muttered darkly. In fact it was a masterpiece. I forgave all when I saw it, and enjoyed many of his subsequent successes - "Black Narcissus" and "The Red Shoes", "The Life and Death of Colonel Blimp", "A Matter of Life and Death" and many others. The Powell/Pressburger partnership spanned a golden age of British film-making.

Another favourite visitor was John Cunningham, the famous night fighter pilot, alias "Cat's Eyes" because of his supposedly miraculous night sight and "Carrots" because of his fondness for the supposedly miraculous vegetables which, according to the Ministry of Food, were responsible for the M.N.S.! Apparently the Ministry had vast stocks of these nourishing roots and were always suggesting new ways of serving them. We boiled, baked, puréed and grated them, made them into cakes and puddings and got heartily sick of them. "Do you really like carrots, John?" I asked him one day. "I absolutely hate the damn things," he replied vehemently. Radar, of course, was his secret, but few people knew it then.

The staff and I were a little apprehensive when Queen Elizabeth's brother, the Hon David Bowes-Lyon and his wife booked a room. We were unaccustomed to mixing with even the outer fringes of the Royal circle, but we needn't have worried. They proved undemanding and charming and sent a two-page 'bread and butter' letter.

People were far more courteous in those days. I received literally hundred of missives from satisfied guests and used to feel a warm glow each time I opened one.

We had started to entertain quite a number of Americans, many of them volunteers from the Eagle Squadron. They were generous to a fault, and bombarded us 'limeys' with candy and cigarettes. The 'thank you' letters went into a drawer on one side of my desk and the 'sweet Caporals' into the other. When I felt depressed, I read a few letters to boost my flagging ego, and when a member of staff felt low, I produced a packet of cigarettes.

I believe the war was won with 'cuppas' and 'cigs' which steadied the nerves in times of stress, and quelled the pangs of hunger when food was short.

Chapter 12 - A Visit from The General

Kerry Harding, when he came on leave, spoke often of General Montgomery; he sounded an interesting fellow, and so when one day a young A.D.C. made a booking for four single rooms for Generals Grassett, Montgomery and aides, I was all agog.

But I made a blunder. "I've only three singles," I said to the two young A.D.C.s when they arrived to inspect the accommodation, "so have put General Grassett in a double one." "Why can't my general have a double room?" complained Monty's aide indignantly. He was an extremely good-looking young man I recollect, so without further persuasion, his general was also allotted a larger room. T'was only fitting, I guess, for the future victor of El Alamein, but at this time he was only on the threshold of his fame. He was a very quiet man. I never heard him address a fellow guest and to me he merely said 'good morning' or 'goodnight'. What, however, he lacked in conversation, he made up for in personal magnetism. One could feel his presence without actually seeing him, an uncanny experience. The two young officers clearly worshipped him, but I suspect the older General Grassett found him a bit of a bore. He neither drank nor smoked, nor even smiled very often. His whole being, mental, physical and spiritual was absorbed by the war, and by his part in the winning of it.

This has often been referred to as the century of the common man. What poppy-cock! This century, like all others, belongs to the Titans, whether good or bad, and Monty was one of them - a good one I like to think. He took command in the desert at a good time logistically. The Army and its equipment had been built up by Auchinleck, but Monty reinvigorated the battle-weary troops with his personal charisma. He supplied the winning ingredients and I feel proud to have met him.

Shortly after Monty's visit, a variety of things happened. The strangest and the most alarming, I suppose, was an invasion alert. The telephone rang very late one night and a curt voice enquired if we had any service people about. "Well, no," I replied. "Then call out the Home Guard and tell them to stand by for further instructions." "Whatever's going on?" I stuttered. "Invasion alert - an unidentified vessel has been seen proceeding in the direction of the Helford River." The phone clicked, leaving me decidedly weak at the knees, but I pulled myself together and ran to rouse

Ronnie. Then I woke Daphne and we seized the binoculars and rushed up to the balcony.

It was eerily quiet, no moonlight but so many stars that the visibility was quite good. "I can't see anything unusual, can you Daphne?" I enquired after a few moments. "Gosh, do you think I should put the sugar in the petrol pump?" "Oh, of course, and sharpen up the carving knives," she replied sardonically. "It's very quiet. I wonder what's happened to the Home Guard?" was my next thought. "You know the Cornish," said my maddening friend. "Ronnie is doubtless making himself a pot of tea." I flew downstairs and sure enough, there in the middle of the kitchen stood a bleary-eyed Ronnie with a mug of tea in his hand. As he went off with a flea in his ear, there was a sudden roar of powerful engines and an Army motor cycle patrol swept into our yard. "Anti parachute patrol," announced a young sergeant. "Have you seen anything suspicious?" "Not yet!" I replied, then held my breath as a solitary aircraft flew overhead. The sergeant looked up and listened. "One of ours," he pronounced. "How do you know?" I mistrusted people who declared they could tell the difference between a Heinkel and a Hurricane. "Training," he replied, adding crushingly, "Jerry would hardly start an invasion with one plane. Where does that lane lead to?" "Bar Beach," I replied, and, rather nastily, "ideal for parachutists." They roared off again, by which time all the guests were aroused. "What the devil's going on?" cried an irate pyjama clad figure from the top of the stairs. "Oh, just an invasion alert," I said as calmly as possible. "Invasion? My God the children!" cried an anguished voice. "Heavens! My pearls!" exclaimed another. "Alas, my sleep," murmured someone else.

Their priorities thus established, guests collected offspring or valuables or went back to bed. A little group of locals hesitated in the porch, hastily clad and clutching battered suitcases. "Should we go to the cellars, miss?" "Er, no," I tried to collect my whirling thoughts. "The cellars are for air raids. You must come in and wait for the coastguard. Ah, here comes the A.R.P. warden." I nearly embraced dear steady old Mr Hewitt and thankfully passed the buck to him. The sight of that little band nearly reduced me to tears as I thought of the empty-eyed refugees at Falmouth the previous year. Mr Hewitt exuded calm. "Nothing new reported so far," he said after 'phoning his A.R.P. post. "Just make yourselves comfortable. The Ladies is up there on the right and the Gents is under the stairs." I blessed his phlegmatic common sense as Mrs Collins lurched towards the cloakroom. "So fear does go to the bowels," I thought. Distraction was urgently needed. "Tea," I said, "we'll make some tea." "That's the least you can do darling," pronounced an actor guest as he descended the stairs in an exquisite Noel Coward dressing gown. "There is absolutely nothing in the brochure about invasions." By the time the L.N.O. arrived, we had quite a party going and I believe there was the slightest tinge of regret when the 'all clear' came.

Next day Commander Warington-Smythe explained what had happened. Out in the bay the Falmouth guard ship had challenged a strange vessel proceeding in our direction. It transpired it was a local patrol boat whose new skipper was not au fait with the Morse Code, so failed to answer the challenge. The guard ship fired a warning shot, and the silly fellow fired back - then scarpered in our direction. "I suppose it gave us good practice should the real thing happen," I suggested, but the L.N.O. would have none of that. "Appalling seamanship!" he thundered. "Do you realise the whole of Plymouth Command was fully mobilised last night? The Navy is the laughing stock of the peninsula!"

Chapter 13 - Farewell My Friend

Not long after this episode, in October 1941, hospital and nursing home could do no more for Angela Harding. She was brought back to the Ferry Boat to die. For Daphne and me, the next few weeks were traumatic. Neither of us had had such a responsibility, and in addition to the running of the Inn, it was indeed a heavy load. The most dreadful part of it was that there was really so little we could do except to administer the morphine which dulled her pain but stole her dignity away. She was constantly sick, and I was at my wit's end, trying to find suitable dishes to tempt her appetite. Despite the open windows and bowls of heavily scented carnations supplied by dear Uncle Bert, nothing could subdue the smell of disinfectant and the awful odour of physical decay. All the staff, particularly Winnie, were wonderfully supportive, the doctor came once a week with morphine, and the District Nurse pedalled down the hill from Mawnan Smith occasionally to help with bedsores. It was heartbreaking, and the distressing memory of that time has left a terrible imprint on my mind. Surely, I thought, there must be better ways of helping people to die?

Many years later, that remarkable woman, Dame Cecily Saunders, has shown the way, and largely inspired by her, the Hospiscare movement has come into being, transforming the care of the terminally ill. But in 1941, in the midst of a world-shattering war, we had to struggle on as best we could; mercifully, in a few weeks my dear friend and mentor was dead.

My remembrances of this tragic episode led me to volunteer for fund raising when Budleigh Salterton and District Hospiscare was founded in 1982. It has proved heart-warmingly successful and now employs three delightful Macmillan Nurses, Ruth Evans, Sue Newby and Liz Gibbons.

There seemed little to be happy about, either at home or abroad. The Japanese had long been at war in the Pacific and were now busily advancing all over the Far East; the Battle of the Atlantic went on remorselessly with terrible losses to the Navy and Merchant Marine, and to our food supplies, while the Luftwaffe were engaged in bombing the main cities all over Britain.

One night Falmouth itself was attacked. We were awakened by the roar of enemy aircraft, wave upon wave of them passing overhead, accompanied by the thunder of the anti-aircraft guns. We tumbled from bed and watched with numbed fascination as the enemy flares turned night into day. Strangely we felt no quaking of the ground which usually accompanied the Plymouth attacks some eighty miles away. From the number of aircraft involved, we feared terrible damage, and were amazed when Mr Hewitt heard via the A.R.P. grapevine that there were practically no casualties. It was extraordinary - how could it be?

Next day we heard the reason. Practically none of the bombs had exploded. From their markings the bomb squads discovered they had been produced in Czechoslovakia, and sabotaged by the slave workers impressed into the armament factories. It was indeed cheering to find that we had these brave but unseen allies working for us in the heart of the Reich. For we were sadly in need of allies, with the French quite out of the war and the Americans not yet in.

We had gained the Russians, of course, when Hitler, in the most extraordinary volte-face, had torn up the Moscow Treaty and invaded Mother Russia. But it was hard to think of the communists as allies, and they were so engaged with the German invasion, there was precious little they could do for us.

The Christmas of '41 is the only wartime one I can remember with any real clarity. Weatherwise it was wonderful. The sun shone from early morning and there wasn't a breath of wind to shatter the mirror-like calm of the water. After the austerity of a wartime Christmas dinner, we went for a river trip and then, as it was still warm and sunny, we had tea on the terrace. The Commander, I recall, took some persuading - he had the usual male aversion to alfresco meals - and an obliging wasp appeared from nowhere to give point to his lamentations; but Kathleen and I were unmoved.

We were in a jubilant mood because at long last, America had declared for the allies. After the surprise attack on Pearl Harbour by the Japanese, I guess President Roosevelt had no option, but it was indeed marvellous news for us. After two hard slogging years we were no longer alone and there was light at the end of the tunnel. No wonder we felt relaxed. The tensions of the past months fell away like the feathers from a chicken in moult. But as always, bad news followed good.

The Japanese, after sinking the Repulse and the Prince of Wales, proceeded on their victorious way, invading Malaya and actually entering Hong Kong on Christmas Day. Their triumphs caused us great anxiety. Brother John had been sent abroad in late autumn, and after enjoying a few happy days of the legendary South African hospitality, had been sent further east. His brigade, we heard afterwards, arrived in Singapore two days before it fell to the conquering Asiatics. The fall of Singapore was a great national and personal tragedy; for my parents a second, traumatic blow.

Then in February '42, the wheel of fortune turned again, and the Americans won a great victory against the Japs in a naval engagement off the Solomon Islands. It was cheering to find out that the enemy in the east was not invincible, and while Canterbury was severely bombed, we were mounting thousand-bomber raids on Germany. Slowly the tides of war began to flow in our favour, and we regained hope.

Chapter 14 - Enchanted Summer

At last the Brittons heard joyous news of their son, Lindsay. He was a District Commissioner in the Gold Coast and was coming on leave. I had heard much of his charm and good looks, but he was bound to be conceited I thought, and was prepared to thoroughly dislike him. However, like everyone else, when we finally met, I found him devastatingly attractive. A stream of friends followed in his wake; most of them stayed at the Ferry Boat and I was delighted to be part of this magic circle.

Uncle Bert, Nora, Reg Green and Lindsay
Helford River

For a few months, life became one long party, a strange counterpoint to the beastliness of war. I wonder I got any work done, with all the gaiety and comings and goings, the capsizings, the 'stuck in the muddings'. Lindsay and Joan Tennant were the first to be marooned. They sailed up to Gweek without checking the tide and spent a night on the mud - just out of reach of Scot's Quay. The Helford is fully tidal, and on the ebb in the upper reaches, the water will suddenly run away like water from an emptying bathtub. They endured much teasing, but unbelievably, a day or two later, George Onslow followed suit. After that, everyone studied the tide-tables!

So that I could join them for cocktails, it became customary for the guests to help prepare the vegetables. We sat on the terrace amongst the beans and sundowners and listened to our colonials and their tales of Africa. Ronnie Haddon was an expert on African art, and he would fetch samples of pottery for us to admire, while Bill Purser talked of his beloved West African riflemen. I couldn't hear enough of the magnificent wildlife and learned all kinds of interesting things about the great animals, the elephants particularly. It seems they have wonderfully endearing habits - when not ruining the crops by taking casual walks through plantations, picnicking as they go. The babies, when tired, sit on treestumps, exactly as they sit on stools in circuses, and at nightfall when all the wild creatures gather at the water-holes, the elephants will spray them all with great trunkfuls of water.

Lindsay had amusing tales of his experiences as a District Commissioner, touring round from village to village, and he spoke of the difficulties of dispensing justice and solving strange native problems with a British legal system. The most usual problems seemed to concern the ownership of oil drums, or the poor quality of cattle supplied for bridal dowries. A very frequent complaint was of "too much mouse shittings in corn" supplied by dishonest merchants. They were happy hours and for a while, the war seemed very far away.

In May 1942, Exeter suffered a series of terrific attacks with incendiary bombs. A little news trickled through, but the telephone lines were down and for several days I couldn't get any news from home. Lord Haw Haw had plenty to say, and although no one trusted him, it was terribly worrying. At last Father telephoned. He had managed to get out of the city and 'phoned from Honiton. All the family were safe and Trelake was undamaged, but all the public utilities were knocked out and large areas of the city utterly devastated. It all sounded horrific, although Father tried to make light of it, and laughed at the difficulties of cooking and boiling water on a solitary Primus stove. Some fires were still raging, the city centre was destroyed, High Street, Sidwell Street, Paris Street, parts of Heavitree, St Thomas and St Davids all reduced to rubble. He said the emergency services had been superb, and my sister Marjory, who was an ambulance attendant, had scarcely slept for days - poor Marjory, she was due to be married in June.

Lord Haw Haw said it was a Baedeker raid. The target was the Cathedral, which was in fact badly damaged but not destroyed, as in Coventry. "Exeter was a jewel and we have destroyed it," Hitler declared triumphantly. What price Cologne? The Germans seemed to think that the loss of our historical monuments would break our "bull-dog" spirit. What strange psychology - it simply made us more furious than ever!

A few weeks later, Marjory's wedding took place as planned, and happily I was able to attend. Had Pop and Marjory not met me at St Davids Station, I doubt I would have got home at all. All the familiar landmarks had disappeared, there was nothing but large piles of black rubble everywhere, some still smouldering, and over all hung a deathly acrid stench.

Blitzed and levelled site of Bedford Circus, c. 1947

The greatest architectural loss was Bedford Circus. That unique jewel of Regency England, a complete circus of elegant houses, was now a burned-out shell. All that remained were gaping facades fronting heaps of black and smelly rubble. The legendary Dellers Cafe with its galleried interior and superb dance floor was completely demolished. Most of the fine High Street shops were either partly or completely destroyed, and many of the ancient little churches, some going back to Saxon times, which had been scattered among the secular buildings, were utterly wrecked. It was terrible to look about, and to see, to smell and to feel the pitiless destruction. Our lovely city, two thousand years in the making, reduced to rubble within a few hours, and with it had gone all the signposts of my childhood.

Fortunately the loss of life was rather less than might have been expected. After some minor raids, most of the inhabitants from the crowded city streets had taken to sleeping in the fields beside the bypass and from there had witnessed the inferno which had engulfed the city and razed their homes. Some survivors told me that they were so thankful to be safe from the blaze that they scarcely gave a thought to their homes at the time.

Astonishingly, the everyday rituals of life went on, and the day after my arrival in the old city, Marjory wed her Walter. Like all wartime weddings, it was a bittersweet affair. The wonder was that the ceremonies went on at all, that the niceties were still observed in those uncertain and barbarous times. We rejoiced for Marjory and hoped she would be happy, but our two missing brothers cast a shadow over us all. Not long after Marjory's wedding, the naval base at Falmouth was abuzz with rumours of a Royal visit. Specific details of these events were never made public for obvious reasons.

Fore Street in the Exeter Blitz, May 1942

Although the carnage out in the Atlantic was terrible, Falmouth Docks had so far escaped relatively lightly from enemy bombing. False markers were laid beyond the Helford to confuse night planes, and many bombs and sea-mines were dropped in that area while the port suffered only lightly. It is only recently that I discovered these 'markers' consisted of false glimmers of light which made the area of the Manacle rocks appear like the blacked-out port of Falmouth. Since the terrible destruction of Plymouth, more and more convoys were routed westward and the Navy and the port workers - apart from the bolshie dockers - worked flat out to keep them moving.

Doubtless people in high places thought some recognition was due. Admiral Thesiger, a small tiger of a man, who was O.C. Falmouth, was very much annoyed. "Surely," he complained bitterly, "we've got enough to do, trying to keep the sea-lanes open, without damn well having to pander to Royalty!"

The great day arrived, and the Commander set off for Falmouth with a twinkle in his eye. "I'll bring the C.O. back for dinner," he said. "I'll lay a sovereign to a tanner he'll have a whale of a time today - he'll be good company tonight!"

How right he was! The two men were positively ebullient when they arrived back that evening. The Admiral was walking on air - "never enjoyed himself so much; the Queen - such beauty, such charm - a word for every man; her visit worth an extra battleship." I'm sure she has never received a finer compliment! "What was she wearing?" we wanted to know. "Oh - a pretty coat and hat." "What colour?" "Pink," said Courtenay. "No, no, mauve," said the Admiral. "Men!" exclaimed Kathleen and I.

Now, more than fifty years later, that gracious, remarkable lady, now the Queen Mother, is still delighting us all.

Gradually the members of the magic circle drifted away, and when the last of his friends had gone, Lindsay often came and helped out on the ferry. To his Mother's intense annoyance, he refused to have his hair cut or indeed to go to Falmouth for anything. I brought back important things like tobacco, "but I can't have your hair cut for you," I expostulated. He got his come-uppance one morning when a cross little woman complained in his hearing that "that lazy old man won't row me over to Helford because he says the tide's too low." When a day or two later he appeared shaven, shorn and beautifully betweeded, I could scarcely believe my eyes. "That woman must have rattled you," I giggled as we walked across the cliffs in the moonlight. "Fraid it isn't that, Nora," he said. "I've got my marching orders. I'm off to Liverpool in the morning."

It was early September. The harvest moon hung low and huge in the sky and was doubled in the still water below. "It's turning awfully chilly," was all I could think of to say. "It's the autumn," he replied. "I've never liked the season of mists and mellow fruitfulness." "But it's a beautiful time - I love it!" I cried. "The fag-end of the year," he said with a desolate note in his voice. "It's the long drawn out death of summer, and I hate it." But it wasn't, I knew, so much the onset of autumn as the passing of an enchanted summer which had brought on his melancholy, and I shivered in the night air as I watched him stride away across the shingle. All the members of the magic circle were scattered about the globe again - Johnnie Spence missing in the Western Desert, Ronnie Haddon tragically, uselessly, dead after a car smash in Africa, Dick Purser back with his magnificent Ashanti warriors, Dick Taylor to his editorial desk in Bristol.

Lindsay was the last to go. The brief, magical summer was gone for ever, lost in the chill air and burnished tints of the "fag-end" of the year.

Peter whined a little. I remember stroking his satiny head, and coming to a sudden decision. "They've all gone now, old chap," I murmured, "and soon, I'm going too. I've really decided now - I'm going to join the W.R.N.S. This time I really mean it."

Well, I was accepted by the W.R.N.S. and left the Ferry Boat at the end of '42. By great good fortune, the Doutons had received an unexpected offer for the Inn so I was able to depart sadly, but without feeling that I had let them down.

Chapter 15 - Killerton, a Tranquil Interlude

The Royal Navy seemed in no great hurry to avail themselves of my services, and at first I revelled in the shedding of responsibility and the luxury of home and leisure. My parents seemed glad to have me, as Freda was now the only one at home; they seemed greatly aged, and my youngest sister had been having a sad time with them. They had borne the loss of Bruce very well, but John's unknown fate cast a terrible shadow over us all, particularly as more details leaked through of the terrible treatment of their prisoners by the Japanese.

John, August 1942

It was a delight to renew acquaintance with old family friends and to observe the quiet support they offered Ma and Pop. A particular friend was Honor Brock, who lived near us with her two small daughters. Honor sadly missed her husband Bill, who was abroad with the Devonshire Regiment, and she had fallen into the habit of spending a post luncheon hour with my parents. She greatly amused them with her nuggets of gossip. As she still had her nanny and a resident maid, she was free to go into Exeter each morning to scrounge around the shops or to carry out her stint of voluntary work; she invariably came back with some scandalous titbit gleaned during the bus journey. "Mrs Ellis is livid!" she told us one day. "Mr Milton, the chemist, told her he had run out of liquid paraffin because housewives are using it for pastry-making! And everyone is buying up the babies' apple purée to use as apple sauce!" The greatest outrage was reserved for some recent arrivals who had sneaked down to Melhuish's market garden at the 'Gallows' and bought up their entire crop of greengages! It had been a point of honour among the locals not to buy too many at once, so that all could have a share. These misfits received scant sympathy when their ancient retainer, in helpful mood, cut up a brand new Chilprufe vest in order to patch an old one!

The city itself, I discovered when on shopping expeditions with Mama, had a strange empty appearance. The City Fathers had thought it imperative for reasons of psychology and hygiene to level the ghastly bomb-sites, and the Council workmen had toiled heroically and carted away all the smelly, rat-infested rubble. There were huge spaces everywhere, already colonised by pink campion - the ubiquitous "fire weed" - which was springing up on bomb-sites everywhere.

Business was carried on in makeshift premises with shored-up walls and boarded windows, few shops or buildings having escaped either complete demolition or minor damage. The whole area presented a scene of aching desolation, and I marvelled at the resilience of the human spirit which kept life ticking over. No one had time for nervous breakdowns and 'disaster counselling' was non-existent. After family tragedies, friends and relations helped to brace each other with a "Let's put the kettle on" or "Come on dear, have one of me cigs and you'll feel much better." To 'whinge' was a social taboo - would that it were so today!

My weeks of freedom were curtailed, not by the Navy but an old school friend, one Joyce Rogers, whose sister Nell was married to John Jacoby. John had a prep school at Robertsbridge; it was called Vinehall; his Mother owned the well-known Battle Abbey School for Girls, and they decided to evacuate the two schools to Killerton Park.

The scheme worked beautifully until old Mrs Jacoby fell ill, and was eventually moved to a new home, taking the school housekeeper to care for her. Joyce rang me up, pleading for help. "I may be called up at any time," I protested, but after several more calls, I eventually agreed to go and try to sort out the domestic shambles.

As any National Trust member knows, Killerton is gracious and welcoming, rather than grand. Centuries of happy family living have endowed its ancient walls with a warm and friendly ambience, and despite its shabby condition I loved the old place on sight. The desks and blackboards looked strange and incongruous in the beautifully proportioned reception rooms, but the flowery-papered bedrooms made homely dorms, and the kitchens were large and bright. The children, the older Battle Abbey girls and the little boys all loved the place and roamed at will in the extensive parkland.

It took a week or two, I recall, to sort out the domestic arrangements. I discovered a gifted cook and several competent kitchen helpers and apart from one rather difficult woman, the cleaning ladies proved to be happy and industrious after their work areas were clearly defined. The difficult lady was propitiated by a chalk line actually drawn across a doorway to mark her boundary - she was an archetypal shop steward disputing the dusting of the few inches of floor between the door jambs!

Soon I was able to relax and started to enjoy myself in the idyllic surroundings. It was good to meet up with Joyce again; I found the Jacobys charming and most of the teaching staff were pleasant. The two school secretaries I liked exceedingly. I can't remember their names but thought of them as "Pen and Ink"; they became particular friends together with the delightful geography teacher, Margaret Savage.

Margaret, Joyce and I often spent time off together, exploring the countryside on our bicycles, or taking the train to Exeter, which entailed cycling to Broadclyst Station where we boarded the train. On one of these occasions fate dealt Margaret a nasty jolt when on the homeward trip her lamp failed. We were stopped by an over-zealous bobby who issued her with a summons - rather ironic I thought when folk like Uncle Bert were summonsed for <u>showing</u> lights! Margaret's case came up during the Easter holidays; she wrote an apologetic note to the Court and enclosed a blank cheque for the expected fine, "but please don't make it more than £2," the letter implored, "or my bank account will be in the red!" The magistrates obliged, but I felt they might have left her a few shillings to the good!

I arrived at Killerton when the grass was swathed in misty clouds of winter cyclamen and dazzling snowdrops. Then came the daffodils and windflowers to herald the glorious pageant of the rhododendrons. Oh, the colour and the perfume! Can any spectacle outshine the unfolding glory of a well-planned rhododendron garden? At Killerton they bloom early, their beauty largely spent by the time the first National Trustees arrive. Azure carpets of bluebells will be there to greet them, but not, alas, the occupants of the old heronry in the trees behind the house. There used to be some twenty mating pairs, and they presented an amusing spectacle with their long legs dangling from one side of their nests and their gangling necks from the other.

The heronry was a favourite haunt of the naturalists, but there were other delights a'plenty. Foxes, rabbits and badgers, toads and hedgehogs, woodpeckers, owls and jays, a regular choir of singing birds and a myriad insects, many examples of which found their way into jars and specimen boxes all around the school.

Less educational than the wildlife but deliciously spooky was the ice cavern, the useful place where ice was stored before the advent of the refrigerator. Sadly this had to be banned after a small boy broke his leg on the slippery steps, but there remained the bear hut; a solemn child assured me that it was constructed of bears' claws. "It would have required a lot of bears," I suggested, but we were both crushed by an owlish little chap who declared that it was made from the bones of many kinds of animals. I expect he was right. Victorians, who constructed so many of these exotic houses, had very curious tastes.

Another favourite leisure spot was the dewpond; surely there are few places more romantic than a dewpond! It is a delight to conjure up visions of the early morning dew-drops cascading down the slopes into the hollowed-out ponds below. My little owlish friend explained the construction in great detail, I remember - like most clever children he felt it his duty to instruct the less well-informed. "You find a depression at the bottom of a slope, and you line it with clay or peat - or even scrunched-up bracken," he explained, "then the dew rolls down the hill and fills it up for the cattle to drink." I suspect these romantic pools owe more to rain than dew-drops but I didn't wish to disenchant my little friend.

The pond has lately been restored, its water piped, its bottom relined, and weeping willows planted around its border. It presents a charming sight but I have a sense of loss. I can no longer imagine the sparkling dew-drops murmuring down the hillside and cascading into the faerie pool below; the mystery has quite gone.

Time passed quickly; the Navy seemed to have forgotten all about me and I became thoroughly engaged with the school and with the pupils - particularly the boys with whom I was in closest contact. My small room was next to one of their dorms, and I used to pop in and out for little chats before "lights out". I got to know them well and was distressed one night to hear the sound of sobbing coming from next door; I crept in to find my little owl in a state of emotional turmoil. He was one of several pupils with divorced parents and I eventually discovered the reason for his grief; though he adored his Father, his Mother, as is usual, had been granted custody, and was actually coming to visit him the following weekend with her new husband. "I don't want another Father," he wept. "I want my own Father and I don't care if I never see my Mother again!"

What words exist to ease such anguish? Joyce had often talked of these children, tossed like flotsam from one parent to another, but this was my first experience of such a case, and I have never forgotten my feeling of inadequacy, as the usual trite comforting words proved useless. "Perhaps we could talk about it tomorrow," I suggested at last, "by the dewpond - I'll get you a nice hot drink now and then we'll meet tomorrow and have a long,

long talk. I still can't quite understand the construction of bear huts and drinking ponds, so we can discuss that as well." I like to think the little chap was comforted, but who really knows what goes on in the minds of children, particularly those from broken marriages?

Apart from these little traumas, the few months spent at Killerton were probably the most peaceful I have ever experienced, forming a tranquil interlude between the hectic Ferry Boat period and the dramatic time spent in the W.R.N.S. Why, even though we were within a mile or two of the airfield at Clyst Honiton and not far from Exeter itself, the sight of an aeroplane crossing the sky gave cause for excitement!

In Cornwall, surrounded by sea, one was ever conscious of the constant battle being fought by the valiant sailors to keep the sea-lanes open. Here we were surrounded by farmers "digging for victory", and all around at harvest time, they worked from dawn to 'dimpsey' bringing in the waves of golden corn which threatened to engulf us.

However, despite the calm, a matter of great consequence was set in motion while I was at Killerton. One morning at breakfast as I admired the garden view through the windows of the dining room, I remarked casually to Joyce how marvellous it would be to see that lovely room restored to its former glory; as we agreed, "Pen and Ink" remembered that Sir Richard would be paying us a visit that day, and shortly afterwards he appeared with a number of sober-suited gentlemen in tow. These chaps toured the estate and poked their noses into every nook and cranny of the house. It was all very mysterious; then, some time later, it transpired they were representatives of the National Trust, and the first steps were taken for the conveyance of the Killerton Estate to the Trust. It was one of the earliest great acquisitions of the Trust in this part of the country, but although generously endowed with land, at the time there was little cash for the necessary repairs and improvements. For many years after the war, when the schools had departed, students from the old St Luke's Training College were in residence. The lovely house became shabbier and shabbier, until at last money was found for its restoration.

I'll never forget the day I entered it, and stood in the dining room once more, struck dumb by its miraculous transformation. Gone were the damp and shabby walls, the faded curtaining, the long rows of wooden tables and benches, and in their stead was set elegant period furniture in an exquisitely refurbished room; for me, a dream had come true.

I spent eight months at Killerton; I celebrated my birthday in September with a party in the bear hut, then shortly afterwards the Navy remembered my existence. In October 1943, once more I boarded the train for Plymouth and began a completely new way of life.

PART III - PLYMOUTH COMMAND

Chapter 16 - Bombed out at Mannamead

After an uneventful journey to Plymouth, I reported to the Initial Training Centre at Mannamead. Within a week we were bombed out, having acquired little but our uniforms and vague notions of galleys, fo'c'sles and liberty boats. It is naval tradition to pretend that land is non-existent, and that all buildings are really ships! We were evacuated to Tamerton Foliot, a gloomy naval camp referred to inevitably as "H.M.S. Portfolio". From there, I was drafted as a cook to Dartmouth.

I had hoped for a complete change and had applied for Operations, but was told the usual tale by the Personnel Officer . "We can quickly train plotters but are desperately short of good cooks," she wheedled. "When you've learned some naval ways, we'll send you on a Mess Caterer's course." "Hmm," I thought sceptically, "there might be more cooks if they were more highly regarded."

On arrival at Dartmouth, I was immediately re-posted to the little fishing town of Beer, where there was an established Radar Station manned by W.A.A.F.s under a single R.A.F. officer. Now a new system had been added which could detect low-flying aircraft and ships, which it was deemed appropriate for the Navy to man. Twelve Wren plotters had been hastily posted thence with a Quarters P.O. in charge. I was to be the cook, and arrived at the commandeered guest house to find them all busily distempering the walls in brilliant white - a Herculean task requiring four coats of paint to obliterate the vivid orange and dark blue which the former proprietors of Sunnyside had thought "such happy colours!"

The next few days were hectic but hilarious; there was little furniture save a bunk bed apiece, a few chairs and a large galley table. Apart from a large tea-pot and a huge kettle I could hardly lift, there were no cooking utensils at all. P.O. had been granted coupons and a messing allowance of twelve shillings per head. "Can you manage on that?" she asked anxiously. "It's generous," I replied. "If we've money for food I'll cook it somehow," and proceeded to make my first ever stew in a kettle. P.O. bought some second-hand utensils out of the messing allowance, and with the enthusiastic support of the tradespeople, we lived like fighting cocks! Eventually, more furniture arrived, and when the redecorating was complete, Sunnyside was the envy of the W.A.A.F.s whom we sometimes invited for tea.

Each morning, Miss Mutter, who ran the local fish cum grocery shop, sent a small boy with a large basket containing vegetables, fresh mackerel, local mushrooms or whatever. "Please ma'am, Miss Mutter says to take what you want and send t'rest back; it'll all be gorn by time y'oum out shopping!" he'd stammer. Such service - we were spoilt indeed! Even the Doctor told P.O. we needn't attend the Sick Parade at the R.A.F. camp as he would come to the Wrennery if necessary.

I have rarely been amongst such a congenial bunch of girls; although from widely differing backgrounds, they all got on well and accepted the initial difficulties with equanimity, and we had all sorts of amusing experiences. I particularly remember the night we missed the last bus from Seaton, after attending the cinema; this was a disaster as Roxana and Pam, two of the plotters, would be in dead trouble if late for night duty. We hitched a lift in the first vehicle that came along, which unfortunately was a fish lorry. The smell hovered round our uniforms for ages!

The little idyll at Beer was of short duration, and soon I was back in Dartmouth, working at Warfleet House, a large damp Wrennery overlooking Warfleet Creek. After promotion to Leading Wren I cooked at the W.R.N.S. Officers' Mess, which entailed a long walk every day; but I asked to remain at Warfleet as I had made some friends there and had a downstairs cabin.

We suffered a 9.30 pm curfew so the downstairs cabin was a boon - one could creep in through the windows much later after arranging for a conspirator to sign the 'In and Out' book. Not that this was often necessary, as there was little social life at first, but I did have an alarming experience one night when returning late from duty. I was walking along the high path towards Warfleet in swirling mist when a drunken American of what seemed <u>enormous</u> bulk loomed out of the fog and put his arm round my waist. "Give us a kiss, honey!" he drawled in an unsteady voice. I couldn't shake him off at first, then aimed a great punch at his middle. The man yelled out and fell onto the road below, while I sped away to sanctuary at Warfleet. It was only later it occurred to me that he might have been injured and I had a sleepless night, imagining I might see a body lying in the road when I went on early duty next morning. Fortunately all was well, but the curfew <u>was</u> designed to get us off the streets before the pubs closed at 10 pm.

Helen Pillar, one of my old Maynard friends, lived in Dartmouth and her family home was a haven of comfort compared with the rigours of the Wrennery. Having lost her Mother at an early age, she ran the home for her Father and the rest of the family, and served in the W.R.N.S. on a daily basis at the Royal Naval College. Life would have been bleak without Helen.

There were few places to meet socially. Dartmouth is a lovely old town but lacked facilities for the ever-increasing number of service people. We found the Raleigh Hotel a pleasant place and met there the crews of the M.G.B.s and newly arrived Yankee P.T. boats. These we teased for their scruffy discipline and though they laughed and pretended not to care, there was a noticeable improvement as the weeks went by. "Gee! H.M.S. Cicala actually saluted us when we dressed ship today," said a young commander proudly one day. (H.M.S. Cicala was Kingswear, across the Dart)

One night, I think it was at the Raleigh, my friend Peggy met Smitty, the commander of a newly arrived L.C.T. Sometimes we were invited aboard his vessel for supper, and these were red-letter days, as our Warfleet diet was appalling. We would look on hungrily as huge rare steaks and piles of chips were flipped straight onto our plates from the grill in the cramped mess cum galley. There would be canned peaches and ice cream and good coffee to follow. After one such ambrosial meal, Smitty remarked, paraphrasing Churchill, that "never in the course of human history had so much food been eaten by so few Wrens!"

The crews of the gallant little M.G.B.s were always very popular. They came and went on their mysterious missions, ferrying secret agents back and forth, collecting beach samples from the French coast to help decide on suitable landing sites. Their exploits have been well-documented in Sir Brookes Richards' official history "The Clandestine Sea Lanes to France and French North Africa." He himself played a large part in both theatres.

There was a steady build-up of the shallow-draught landing craft specially designed as carriers of troops and equipment, which could float almost straight onto the invasion beaches. They were moored up-river, close in to the tree-lined banks which afforded natural camouflage to confuse reconnaissance aircraft. The villages of Strete and Torcross were evacuated so that the great expanse of Slapton Sands could be used for mock landing exercises using live ammunition. Not surprisingly, but very sadly for their owners, few houses survived. It was common to see the vessels set out and return from these manoeuvres, but one day only a few returned by sea and streams of ambulances poured into town. 'U' boats had penetrated the convoys, causing great loss of ships and lives; it was chilling to have such a happening so close to home, and pitiful to see so many shell-shocked young Americans about the town, until they were scooped up by the medicos.

As spring advanced, the Yanks took over the Royal Naval College, removing all the doors and driving their jeeps through the hallowed portals, to the fury of the local populace. The hospital was also commandeered, then they set about enlarging the quay, erecting huge floodlights so they could work by night as well, in the usual "gung ho!" American fashion.

Chapter 17 - D Day

By late spring we woke up to the fact that Dartmouth was to play an important part in the forthcoming invasion; tension mounted as the whole area was placed under a news blackout; no mail or telephone calls were allowed, all leave was stopped and all social visiting to ships was strictly forbidden. By the beginning of June, the new 'Hard' was ready, and on the 4th, a great convoy of landing craft was quietly brought down-river; they had been so well concealed by the tree-hung banks we had had no idea there were so many - over three hundred and fifty in all - of these large, ingenious craft, so cleverly designed for storming beaches, but notoriously unstable at sea because of their flat bottoms. As the ships took up their stations, an endless stream of infantry, tanks and armoured vehicles began to rumble through the ancient streets of Dartmouth to the newly enlarged quayside.

The planning was immaculate. The appropriate vessels were brought to the quayside as their allotted units arrived for embarkation, and when full, they returned to their stations and the next wave took their places. I spent all my spare time as near the scene of operations as I dared, (the whole area was forbidden territory, of course) and I marvelled at the precision of it all as frenetic manifest officers matched men and machines to their allotted transports. (I suppose they were the forerunners of the roll-on ferries). At last, after twenty-four hours of hectic activity, the quay was empty and eerily quiet, all the laden vessels quietly anchored in long lines midstream. There was no doubt this was no rehearsal, but the real thing. Operation Overlord, the long planned invasion of Europe, was upon us at last.

Forty-eight hours later, the landing craft were still riding at anchor. A storm-force gale was raging in the Channel, making it nigh on impossible for the unseaworthy vessels to venture out. It was generally known that the troops could only be held aboard for seventy-two hours, so by Saturday pm, time was rapidly running out. The gale still raged, and the perfect conjunction of moon and tide would not re-occur for weeks. It was a nerve-wracking period, and a numb feeling of anticlimax engulfed all the Wrens at Warfleet as we drifted off to bed on the Saturday night.

Early next morning, one of the watch-keepers rushed excitedly into our cabin. "Wakey wakey!" she cried. "It's started! The invasion is on after all!" "But what about the weather?" The gale has abated a little, but all hell's been let loose in the Channel, and bombs are dropping like hailstones all down the French coast!" "I thought I heard aircraft!" cried someone as we scrambled into our clothes, all chattering at once. "Where are they landing?" "Hard to say yet - diversions all over the place, but the main thrust seems to be Normandy." "Gosh, what a terrible decision for Ike - he must have thought 'now or never'," we all thought as we raced to the bottom of the garden. We had a grandstand view of the estuary from Kingswear to the river mouth, but nothing moved for a long time. I felt sick with apprehension and a kind of suppressed excitement, when at length we noticed some movement. The little flotilla of M.G.B.s, immaculate and disciplined as ever, proudly led the great procession, closely followed by the P.T. boats; then came the scores and scores of landing craft with their accompanying frigates. Such a fabulous spectacle had never been witnessed at Dartmouth before, or was ever likely to be seen again, though it suddenly occurred to me that nearly four hundred years previously, local people had watched from the nearby cliffs the stately galleons of the Spanish Armada being harried along the coast by the English fleet, under Effingham and Drake. History repeats itself, though never in quite the same way, or on quite the same scale, but perhaps it was a good omen.

Meanwhile, with tears streaming down our faces, we waved and sang and cheered this present day Armada until the last ships disappeared from view to join the even greater gathering in the Channel. How many would survive, we wondered? Indeed, would the great enterprise succeed? It was the last throw of the dice, for such a mammoth force could never be re-assembled in secret, and if it failed, the future would be bleak indeed. We were all very subdued for the rest of that day.

Chapter 18 - Teignmouth

After D Day, the war moved away from Dartmouth and most of us were redrafted. I was summoned one day by First Officer Fubini, our attractive and recently acquired 'Queen Bee'. "I've been looking at your records," she said briskly. "H.M.S. Mount Stewart is being reorganised. They need a Mess Caterer and I am recommending you." I was surprised and delighted, then recalled with dismay that I hadn't been on an M.C. course. "I don't think we need worry about that," she said, "considering your previous experience," and added with a sly grin, "I expect you've discovered a galley is a kitchen! You will be made up to Petty Officer of course. A transport leaves for Teignmouth at 0800 hours tomorrow!" I could have kissed her! A proper job at last, and a tricorn hat! "And £2 a week," added my Warfleet friends as they helped me pack. Yes, that was a consideration. Ordinary W.R.N.S. got only seven shillings and Leading W.R.N.S. £1 - out of which many fine girls from poor families sent home at least half. I think that is unlikely to happen these days.

The 'Wrennery' at Teignmouth was pleasantly comfortable compared with the damp and chilly Warfleet, but I found I spent little time there except for sleeping; my future life was to centre round the Officers' Mess sited in a former hotel named Glendaragh, and here I found absolute chaos. From the departing Mess Caterer, I gathered that an invasion fleet had gone out from Teignmouth and that a complete new unit was taking over the base. "I hope you can cope," she said gloomily. "There's no food and no money." "And no doors," I observed. "You must have had Americans here as well!" "Oh yes, the doors are all piled up in the outhouses but the 'chippies' are coming to fit them tomorrow. The Quarters P.O. is here; her stewards are preparing the cabins for the new intake, and trying to get the Wardroom into some sort of order." I gathered I would have to draw main supplies from the N.A.A.F.I., once the documentation was sorted out, and "extras" would be paid for by the Officers and debited on their monthly Mess bills; I asked for a list of the local suppliers of these "extras", and for the whereabouts of "No. 1" who would be in overall charge of Glendaragh. She produced this information then said she was "off", and I departed in search of the First Lieutenant.

He was at the Royal Hotel, half of which had been commandeered by the Navy for its H.Q. He proved very helpful; apparently I was also to be responsible for the Captain's Mess, which was a separate establishment.

After much telephoning and issuing of permits and accreditations etc, I made myself known at the N.A.A.F.I., and arranged for preliminary supplies. I then visited the Teignmouth shops and begged for a little credit until the new officers arrived, as I wished to greet them with acceptable meals. The kindly shopkeepers were very happy to oblige; they all became my friends and were invariably helpful, except for an elderly lady who ran a chemist's shop. She couldn't supply me with certain very important female necessities she said, because she knew that 'service women had them supplied free'. Well, we certainly didn't get them in the W.R.N.S., and in desperation I had to appeal to our W.R.N.S. officer to give me a memo to that effect before she would oblige me!

Meanwhile, I was summoned by our C.O., the distinguished, bearded Captain Brunton. This was his first shore command and he seemed slightly bemused by female sailors. He ran a tight ship, he said, couldn't stand sloppy standards, a disciplined ship meant a happy one, etc etc. It was quite obvious that his bark was worse than his bite and after a few days, he relaxed into a good humoured but very efficient officer, and a kindly, courteous man. He had many official visitors, and always sent a courier with a letter of thanks after special events. One of these couriers was a marine corporal named Gordon Ingram-Marriott who had the looks of a young Viking and was destined to be my future husband.

One of Captain Brunton's guests, to my astonishment, proved to be the Captain Slocum who used to visit the Helford flotilla. From his accompanying aide I discovered that the mysterious man was in fact an Admiral, none other than the Deputy Head of Operational Naval Intelligence. Gerard Holdsworth's unit, as I had surmised, <u>had</u> been running a clandestine boat service to France, and besides ferrying agents, had rescued many allied airmen, and carried out many hazardous operations.

Gordon Ingram-Marriott, Teignmouth, 1945

Pierre Guillet, who used to frequent the bar at the Ferry Boat, was the owner of a French tunnyman which had been captured by a British submarine; he agreed to help the S.O.E. 'Mutin' had been acquired by Gerry and fitted with a powerful captured German diesel engine. Under

Pierre's guidance, 'Mutin' used to mix with the Brittany tunny fishing fleet to pick up intelligence information, and also to transfer arms and radios etc to genuine French fishing boats for landing in France. (Pierre is still alive and is Mayor of his home town in France). I also learnt that the original Helford flotilla had gone to North Africa with Commander Holdsworth and was doing sterling work out there. Brookes Richards was his second-in-command and a brilliant Arabic linguist. In Arabian disguise, he picked up a lot of useful information about the Germans. The Warington-Smythe brothers, Nigel and Bevil, were by that time running the Helford unit and liaising with the Dartmouth M.G.B.s. I felt quite dizzy with all these revelations; I felt I had been going around in a circle! I wondered aloud how Captain Slocum fitted into the H.M.S. Mount Stewart operation. Because, I was informed, it was being used as a preparation base for secret operations against Japan. The Royal Marines used weapons and techniques largely inspired by the legendary Blondie Haslar, and were testing out specially evolved secret craft; I remember the motorised submersible canoes (M.S.C.s), Major Haslar's particular "baby", also the motor flotation units (M.F.U.s), the midget submarines and an optimistic submersible with a time clock, which could be primed to pop up for a returning raiding party to take them home. The European offensive was well advanced and now the British had to prepare to support the Americans in their great planned assault on the Japanese mainland.

Mount Stewart was run by the Navy under the afore-mentioned Captain Slocum. I remember the young New Zealander, Chuck Ardell, and Lieutenant Harry and Sub-Lieutenant Grace, scarcely out of school. There were three senior officers whose names escape me, though one was much teased because he looked like Friar Tuck. Our M.O., Dr Jamieson, became a great friend. He was a volunteer from Southern Ireland, and a pacifist. "I couldn't take life," he said, "but I have been trained to save life, and this is my way of fighting tyranny."

There were several Army officers, a Flight Lieutenant and sundry American observers, but the main force was composed of Royal Marines from the Royal Marine Boom Defence Patrol - a euphemism to cover their secret activities - under Major Bill Pritchard-Gordon. I remember the young Lieutenants, Stan Hurst, Peter Davies, John Arnold and David Cox among others - and I mustn't forget the dogs which always seemed to end up in my custody. The canine star of Glendaragh was Nadine, a magnificent St Bernard, who caused a minor sensation when I took her shopping one day. She enjoyed all the attention so much she refused to let me out of the door next day without her and I had to exit from the office window!

I got caught up in the atmosphere of Mount Stewart. Peace reigned in the Mess (except for the monthly Mess nights!) and there was a wonderful spirit of camaraderie between officers and other ranks, whilst Wrens moved

*Right: Shopping with Nadine,
Teignmouth, 1944*

*Below: R.M.B.D.P. at sea,
Teignmouth, 1945*

freely between them all. My best Wren friends were "Dame" Thomas, who was the Captain's driver, and Brita Cedarström and Audrey (?) who were attached to Glendaragh. Sometimes we had cocktails with young officers at the Royal Hotel, and at others, I joined Gordon and his Marine pals at a local pub. I particularly liked the Marine Sergeants, Taffy Evans and Lofty Moorhouse. Gordon and I often joined them and their girl friends, but increasingly we tended to go about on our own, exploring the Teign estuary on foot, or sometimes in a purloined canoe or rowing boat. Gordon was a wonderful dancer, and we went to all the local hops and learned to jive with the best of them. Happy days indeed, when the war in Europe and the Pacific seemed very far away. We had to make the best of the happy times, for the men frequently disappeared to Fort William or the Shetlands for missions or special training. I learned much later that during the winter of '44, Lieutenant Hurst, with Taffy and Gordon, had prepared in terrible weather conditions for a 'U' boat raid on Norway; their gear had already been stowed aboard a support vessel when the raid was suddenly aborted, due to the appalling weather. Gordon never mentioned it. Secrecy was absolute.

Of course, my life didn't consist entirely of dancing and carousing! In fact I was kept very busy. Despite the excellent cooks at both establishments, I had to check the stores and oversee the kitchens, make sure all the meals were served on time and that emergency meals were always available. I would then visit the N.A.A.F.I. and scour the shops for the so important extras, and hunt for flowers in the Glendaragh garden with which

Members of R.M.B.D.P. outside Courtenay House, 1944

to adorn the Mess tables. It always surprised and pleased me to find how much these macho men appreciated these little niceties.

There was a great deal of paperwork, and also responsibility for the drinks locker and the cigarette rations; it was my unpleasant duty to inform junior officers when they had reached their monthly quota of drinks, a rule strictly enforced to prevent them running up large Mess bills they could ill afford. Every tot was entered in the wine and spirits book which was inspected by Captain Brunton at regular intervals. "Oh, Mess," (as I was inelegantly named), "I couldn't <u>possibly</u> have drunk all that!" was a frequent lament, or "are you <u>sure</u> you haven't any extra cigarettes, Mess? I lost my last lot in the drink yesterday!" This was generally Nigel Harry. I had a soft spot for him - he always looked very ill, having spent a long tour of duty on the ghastly Russian convoys. The watch-keepers on these convoys used to take pills to keep awake and often went without sleep for several days and nights, due to the constant attacks from the 'U' boats and enemy aircraft. Half the convoys would be lost before they reached Murmansk, to a sullen reception from the Russians who never said "thank you," but "why haven't you brought us more?" Lieutenant Harry usually got his extra cigarettes.

The war in Europe ended in May 1945. I can still hear the joyous tumult of the church bells ringing out for victory; I can remember tearing down the blackout curtains, and, most moving of all, when travelling by train from Exeter that night, I can still see in my mind's eye the entire coastline ablaze with bonfires, their leaping flames reflected in the sea. Flames, not of destruction this time but flames of celebration for the end of phase one of this dreadful world-wide conflict.

As peace came to Europe, the war in the East intensified. Tension mounted as the Marines' training reached its apogee, and by early July, the whole unit at H.M.S. Mount Stewart was put on standby for the Pacific.

Gordon and I decided to get married. "Oh Nora, is it wise to marry just now?" sighed my Mother. "Probably not," I replied, "but how can one be sensible at times like these? It will be a miracle if Gordon survives these operations in the Far East." We were wed within the week.

Mother arranged a lovely wedding. Captain Brunton lent his car and his driver Jane, the future Duchess of Somerset. Half the base turned up at the Church of All Saints, Whipton, and after a reception in the garden at home, Gordon and I departed for a three day honeymoon at the Carnarvon Arms at Dulverton.

The three days lengthened into six, then nine, by which time we were dead broke and had to return home. Embarkation orders had still not been received by the time we returned to Teignmouth. It was a strange uneasy time; Gordon and I were in daily, even hourly, expectation of being parted, and I set off on a messing trip one morning feeling very gloomy indeed.

Gordon and Nora, July 1945

When I returned, Doc Jamieson hailed me from the doorstep of Glendaragh. He was in a state of tremendous excitement. "What is it?" I cried. "Has the war ended?" "Not yet," he replied, "but it won't be long. They've dropped an atom bomb on Hiroshima, and the result is so terrible, it will be the end of war in our time. Certainly the end of this one and of all major wars in future!"

It was wonderful news, which had spread like wildfire, and soon I was ambushed for the keys of the drinks locker. All the officers and all the Wrens had assembled in the wardroom. Even as we celebrated, news came of the second bomb on Nagasaki and the consequent surrender of the Japs. I wonder the roof stayed on Glendaragh, with all the shouting, the cheering, the singing and general exuberance.

The war was over - there would be no assault on Japan with the expected 90% casualties. Gordon and all the Marines had been saved, all the unit had been saved, all the tens of thousands of British troops in Asia had been spared, and the hundreds of thousands of American allies who had been engaged in the Far East operations. The atom bomb had succeeded, and though a terrible weapon, had saved countless lives and possibly years of further suffering. Doc Jamieson was right - he was a pacifist but a realist. It was unlikely that anyone would begin a major war in the foreseeable future; for after two thousand years of Christian teaching, fear, it seems, is still much stronger than love. I find that unutterably sad.

THE END